DATE DUE			
OCT 19 99			
NOV 4 00			
FEB 14 01			
DEC 14 01			
OCT 2 7 2003			
APR 19 2006			
MAR 2 0 2007			
MAR 2 2 2012			

Mississippi

Mississippi

Charles George and Linda George

Children's Press®
A Division of Grolier Publishing
New York London Hong Kong Sydney
Danbury, Connecticut

Frontispiece: Passenger steamer

Front cover: The state capitol

Back cover: One of Mississippi's many waterfalls

Consultant: Dr. John Ray Skates

Please note: All statistics are as up-to-date as possible at the time of publication.

Visit Children's Press on the Internet at http://publishing.grolier.com

Book production by Editorial Directions, Inc.

Library of Congress Cataloging-in-Publication Data

George, Charles.
    Mississippi / by Charles George and Linda George.
        144 p. 24 cm. — (America the beautiful. Second series)
    Includes bibliographical references and index.
    Summary : Describes the geography, plants and animals, history, economy, language, religions, culture, and people of the state of Mississippi.
        ISBN 0-516-20688-5
        1. Mississippi—Juvenile literature. [1. Mississippi.] I. George, Linda. II. Title.
    F341.3.D38 1999
    976.2—dc21   98-19618
                                                                                         CIP
                                                                                          AC

Acknowledgments

The authors wish to thank the following people for their help in securing research materials for this book: Governor Kirk Fordice and staff; Senator Thad Cochran and staff; Senator Trent Lott and staff; Mississippi Department of Tourism; Mississippi Department of Archives and History; the chambers of commerce throughout the state; and the staff of the USS *Cairo* Museum. A special thanks goes to Mary Elizabeth Cox, docent of the governor's mansion in Jackson, for her gracious help during our visit. Many thanks to everyone else we met and spoke to while we were in Mississippi for helping us to write the best book possible—and for making us feel right at home.

Oak trees

The Lady Luck
Riverboat Casino

The Mississippi Delta

Contents

Magnolia blossom

Stanton Hall

Jackson

Mardi Gras celebration

Mockingbird

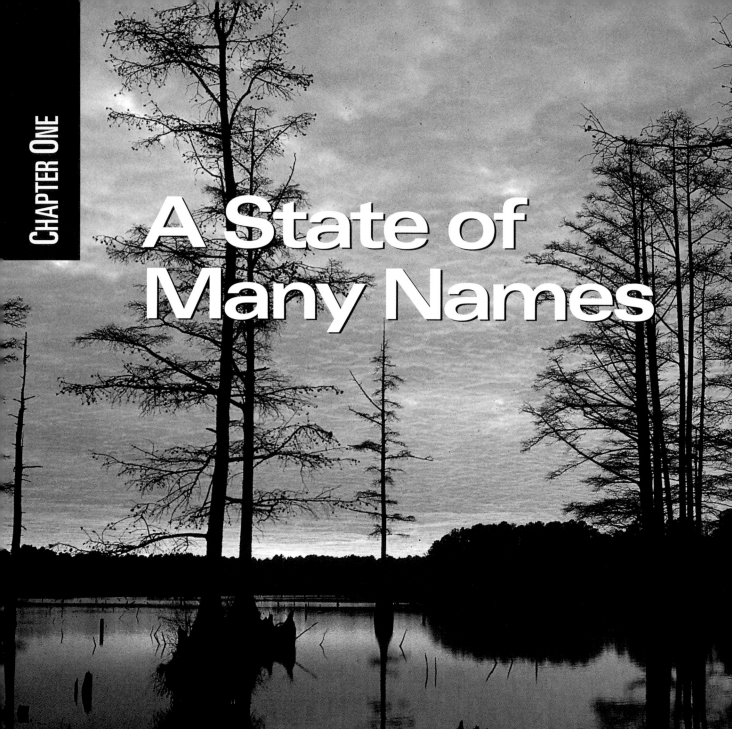

CHAPTER ONE

A State of Many Names

Mississippi is known for its beautiful natural settings.

The state of Mississippi is named for the great river that forms its western boundary. The state might very well have been named Greenland, however, for the many shades of green that fill its interior.

Green is the color of the Mississippi's many trees, pastures, rice paddies, and cotton fields. It is the color of the large, dark leaves of the state tree, the magnolia, which gives the state its nickname— the Magnolia State—and whose snowy-white blossoms are the state flower. Green is also the color of kudzu, the vine that grows everywhere—and that some folks jokingly say is trying to eat the South. In addition to the green of its agricultural and natural plant life, Mississippi displays the greens of golf courses, manicured lawns, and the felt surfaces of gaming tables. As the state continues to add new industries, modern highways, luxury hotels, and resorts, it adds yet another shade of green—the green of money and prosperity.

Opposite: Cypress trees at sunset

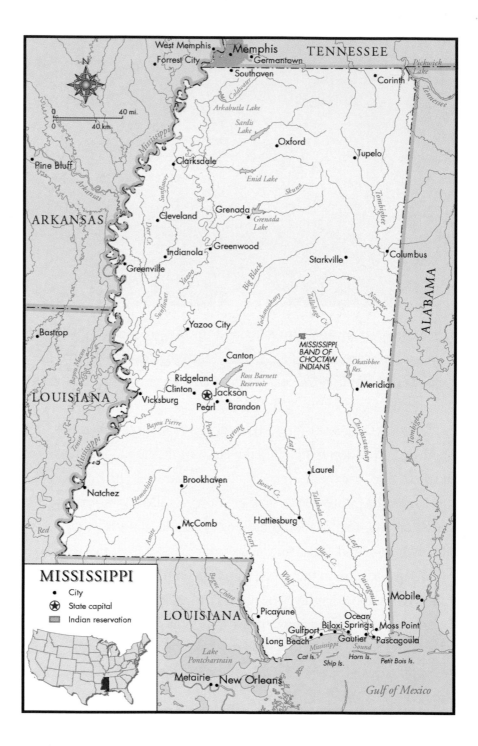

MISSISSIPPI
- • City
- ★ State capital
- ▨ Indian reservation

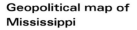

Geopolitical map of Mississippi

The River with Many Names

The state of Mississippi was named for the Mississippi River, which flows along the region's western boundary. The river was given different names by the various Native American tribes who lived near its banks or traveled its waters.

The Ojibwa tribe called the river *mici zibi,* which means "gathering in of all the waters." The Choctaw called it *mish sha sippukrie,* which means "father of waters" or "beyond age." The Algonquins named it *messipi,* which means "big river." ■

The color green is also symbolic of life and growth, and nowhere is growth more evident than in Mississippi. The state has a long, rich heritage. Its past is filled with happiness and achievement, but also with strife and despair. In recent years, however, Mississippi has become one of the most forward-thinking, progressive states in the United States. Although Mississippians will never forget their traditions—or the trouble and triumphs of their past—they are moving toward a bright and prosperous future.

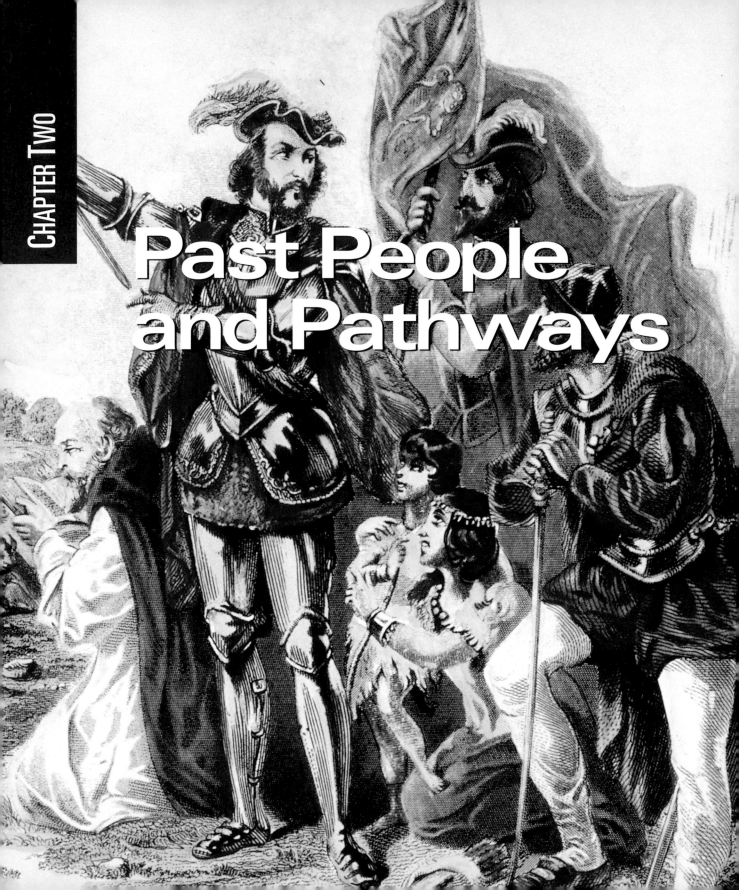

CHAPTER TWO

Past People and Pathways

Emerald Mound

Some scientists believe that nomadic people arrived in the land that is now Mississippi about 12,000 years ago. The ancestors of these people crossed a land bridge into North America from present-day Siberia. That strip of land is now submerged beneath Alaska's Bering Strait.

These early Mississippians left no written records. Archaeologists learn about them from the bones of the animals they ate and the remains of their tools and weapons. Prehistoric people also left pottery and clay utensils. Some of these interesting artifacts have been found near huge, man-made mounds of earth throughout Mississippi.

Scientists are not sure why the early inhabitants of this part of North America built mounds. The mounds could have been built to escape flood waters. They could also have been used as platforms from which to send signals. A few mounds show evidence of stockade fences, and probably served as forts.

Archaeologists have unearthed clay pots, masks, and engraved seashells on several Mississippi mounds. These discoveries suggest that some mounds served as foundations for important buildings, such as temples. Some of the many mound sites scattered across the

Opposite: Explorer Hernando de Soto on the shore of the Mississippi River

Emerald Mound

Emerald Mound, the largest of the prehistoric mound sites found in Mississippi, covers 8 acres (3.2 ha) near the city of Natchez. It was the only North American mound site that was still occupied by Native Americans when European explorers arrived in the early eighteenth century. The written reports of some early French visitors help scientists today interpret the artifacts uncovered at Emerald Mound and at other mounds in the United States.

The excavations at Emerald Mound have revealed stone axes, spades, hoes, clay cups and bowls, and mortars and pestles for grinding corn. Early inhabitants also left carvings of people and animals, which were probably used in games or religious ceremonies. Some of the most remarkable of these carvings appear on calumets, or peace pipes. ▪

state are the Lake George Site near Yazoo City, Emerald Mound near Natchez, and the Winterville Mounds north of Greenville.

Native Mississippians

By the early sixteenth century, three major Indian tribes—the Chickasaw, Choctaw, and Natchez—ruled the area that is now Mississippi. The Chickasaw lived in the north, and the Choctaw lived in the central part of the state. The Natchez, who are thought to be descendants of the mound builders, lived in the southwest along the Mississippi River.

The Chickasaw were brave, independent, and warlike. Their villages were strong and well situated, sometimes stretching in a long line for miles. Because of the Chickasaw's strength and their well-organized society, their enemies were seldom able to capture them.

The Choctaw were powerful but peaceful, fighting only when necessary. They farmed and traded, and their villages were strong, compact, and fortified. Their tribal government was a democracy with a constitution, elections, and courts to settle legal questions. The Choctaw were called Flats or Flatheads by the early European traders; neighboring tribes called them Long Hairs. The Choctaw considered their long hair and sloping, flat foreheads as signs of distinction. They flattened the heads of male babies by pressing boards against the babies' foreheads soon after birth.

The pottery of the Natchez Indians

The Natchez were one of the few tribes in North America whose chiefs had complete power over their subjects' lives and property. In their society, there were rigid class distinctions. Three levels of nobility—the highest were the Suns—ruled the Natchez. The commoners were known as Stinkards. The Natchez believed that their chief, the Great Sun, was a descendant of the Sun God. The chief was carried everywhere on a special litter so that his feet never touched the ground. When the Great Sun died, his wife and all his Stinkard servants were strangled and buried with him as part of a great funeral ceremony.

The Chickasaw, Choctaw, and Natchez held power over numerous smaller groups. The Chakchiuma, Tunica, Taposa, Ibitoupa, Tiou, Ofo, and Yazoo tribes lived along the Yazoo River. The Biloxi, Acolapissa, and Pascagoula tribes inhabited the Gulf Coast. The Houma lived in the southwest corner of the state. About 25,000 to 35,000 Native Americans were living in the Mississippi region when the first European explorer, Hernando de Soto, arrived in 1540.

The Early Explorers

Hernando de Soto was the first European to visit Mississippi. While serving as Spanish governor of Cuba, he heard about a "land of gold" and decided to lead an expedition north to find it. In May 1539, de Soto and his 600 men landed on the gulf coast of Florida. They meandered across land that later became the states of Georgia, South Carolina, North Carolina, Tennessee, and Alabama. In 1540, de Soto and his men crossed into what is now the state of Mississippi. They entered from the east, about 8 miles (13 km) north of the present-day town of Columbus.

In May 1541, de Soto became the first European to see the Mississippi River. Crossing the great river, he and his men continued through Arkansas and Louisiana. They returned to the Mississippi River somewhere along the Louisiana bank, across from the site of present-day Natchez. There, de Soto died from a fever, and his men buried him in the river. De Soto's men left the area without finding gold or establishing any settlements.

Father Jacques Marquette and Louis Jolliet led a group of French explorers into Mississippi in 1673.

A group of seven French explorers visited Mississippi in 1673. They were led by Father Jacques Marquette, a Jesuit missionary, and Louis Jolliet, a fur trapper. The men traveled from the Great Lakes to the point where the Arkansas River joins the Mississippi River, near what is now the town of Rosedale. After a brief encounter with a local tribe—probably Chickasaw or Choctaw—the men returned to Canada.

In 1682, the French explorer René-Robert Cavelier, Sieur de La Salle, journeyed down the Mississippi River from Canada to the Gulf Coast. He claimed for France all the land drained by the river. La Salle named the region Louisiana in honor of France's king, Louis XIV.

French Settlement

In 1698, King Louis XIV commissioned Pierre Le Moyne, Sieur d'Iberville, to occupy the region known as Louisiana. In 1699, d'Iberville entered Mississippi from the Gulf Coast, near the site of present-day Biloxi. He established the first permanent settlement, Fort Maurepas, at what is now Ocean Springs. Fort Maurepas became the first capital of the vast French colony on the North American continent.

In 1716, d'Iberville's brother, Jean Baptiste Le Moyne, Sieur de Bienville, established a second French settlement at Fort Rosalie, the site of modern Natchez. There, French colonists built plantations to raise cotton, tobacco, rice, and indigo, a plant used to

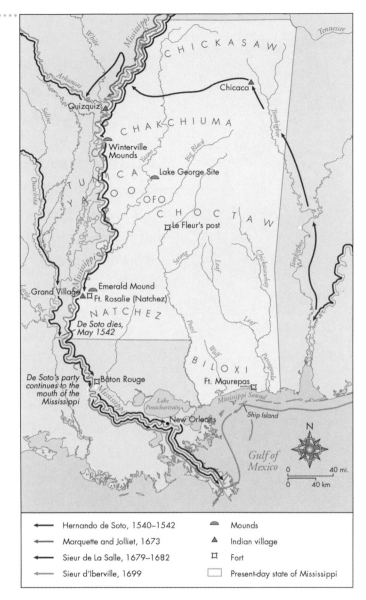

Exploration of Mississippi

King Louis XIV of France

make blue dye. In 1719, the first black slaves were transported from Africa to work in the plantation fields. The French maintained control over the area for more than sixty years.

English and Spanish Rule

After being defeated by the British in the French and Indian War in 1763, France lost its vast colonial empire. The British gained all the land east of the Mississippi River, except New Orleans. The southern portion of Mississippi became part of the British province of West Florida. The northern portion joined the British colony of Georgia.

During the American Revolution (1775–1783), most settlers in West Florida remained loyal to the British. Those in Georgia supported the American colonists. In 1781, while the British were at war, Spain took control of West Florida without opposition.

Two years later, in 1783, Great Britain lost the Revolutionary War. The British government officially granted West Florida to Spain. England's land north of 32° north latitude became part of the newly formed United States. On October 27, 1795, the Treaty of San Lorenzo el Real established the border between the United States and Spanish West Florida at the 31st parallel (31° north latitude). Today, that border forms part of the boundary between the state of Mississippi and Louisiana.

Mississippi Territory

On April 7, 1798, the U.S. Congress established the territory of Mississippi with Natchez as its capital. The territory was bounded on the west by the Mississippi River and on the east by the Chattahoochee River. The northern boundary extended east from the mouth of the Yazoo River. The southern border was the 31st parallel. In 1804, Congress extended the Mississippi Territory north to the border of Tennessee.

In August 1798, U.S. president John Adams appointed Winthrop Sargent as the territory's first governor. In 1801, Sargent asked the Choctaw and Chickasaw for permission to build a road through their lands. The road would link Nashville, Tennessee, to Natchez and would provide an overland route for people returning from trips down the Mississippi River. The road, which was 450 miles (720 km) long, was to follow the old Natchez Trace, a path long used by American Indians. Today, the Natchez Trace Parkway, which closely follows the course of the original Natchez Trace, is both a scenic highway and a national park.

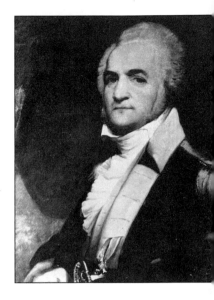

In 1798, Winthrop Sargent was appointed the first governor of the Mississippi Territory.

Republic of West Florida

After the United States purchased the Louisiana Territory from France in 1803, the Mississippi River opened to U.S. commerce. The Gulf Coast from New Orleans east to Florida, however, was still under Spanish rule. Conflicts erupted between Spanish officials and Florida settlers. In one incident in 1810, about one hundred American settlers captured the Spanish fort at Baton Rouge, Louisiana.

The settlers declared themselves the Republic of West Florida. The republic included the area of Spanish West Florida south of the 31st parallel, from the Mississippi River east to the Perdido River, near the present-day city of Pensacola, Florida. In 1812, the area of the West Florida Republic east of the Pearl River was added to Mississippi Territory.

During the War of 1812, Major General Andrew Jackson led the U.S. forces, which included many Mississippians, in the defeat of the British.

The War of 1812

Because of trade conflicts, on June 18, 1812, the United States declared war on Great Britain. Most of the battles took place around the Great Lakes and along the northern Atlantic coast of the United States. After more than two years of fighting, both sides signed the Treaty of Ghent, officially ending the war on December 24, 1814.

News of the peace treaty, which was signed in Ghent, Belgium, did not reach the United States for several weeks. The Battle of New Orleans, one of the major battles of the War of 1812, was fought on January 8, 1815—fifteen days after the war officially ended. Major General Andrew Jackson led a force of men that included hundreds of Mississippians and defeated the British forces. Nearly one thousand Choctaw warriors, led by Choctaw chief Pushmataha, fought alongside Jackson for the United States in the battle.

Statehood

By 1813, the Mississippi Territory included all of present-day Mississippi and Alabama. Two years earlier, territorial governor

Chief Pushmataha

Pushmataha (1764?–1824) was chief of the Choctaw tribe in central Mississippi. In the War of 1812, Pushmataha fought as a colonel alongside General Andrew Jackson during the Battle of New Orleans. Jackson called Pushmataha "the greatest and bravest Indian" he ever knew.

Twelve years after the battle, Pushmataha traveled to Washington, D.C., to discuss American settlements on Choctaw lands. While in Washington, the chief became ill with diphtheria and died. Pushmataha was given a funeral with full military honors and buried in the Congressional Cemetery in Washington, D.C.

David Holmes had begun pushing for statehood. In 1817, the U.S. Congress finally divided the Mississippi Territory into the state of Mississippi, with its current boundaries, and Alabama Territory.

In the summer of 1817, a constitutional convention met in the village of Washington, Mississippi, to write a state constitution. On October 17, David Holmes officially became Mississippi's first governor. On December 10, 1817, Mississippi entered the union as the twentieth state, with Natchez as its capital.

According to a census in 1817, a few free blacks, 23,000 black slaves, and 25,000 whites lived in Mississippi. The American Indian population was not included in the census. Historians today, however, estimate that 35,000 American Indians lived in the newly formed state and controlled two-thirds of its land.

Between 1817 and 1822, the towns of Natchez, Washington, and Columbia served as state capitals. In 1822, the new capital, Jackson, was built on the site of Le Fleur's Bluff, a frontier trading

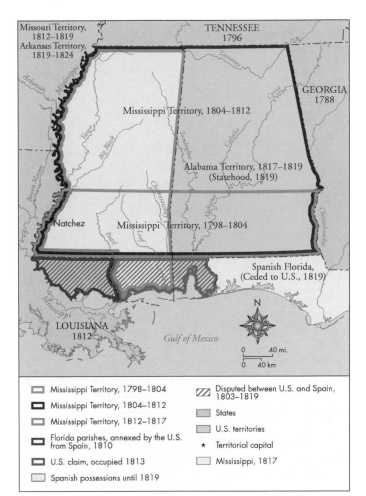

Historical map of Mississippi

Native Americans had an important presence in early Mississippi and continued to live there and control land into the 1800s.

post on the Pearl River. The town was named in honor of Major General Andrew Jackson, known as the Hero of the South.

Land Treaties

As more and more settlers arrived in Mississippi, local tribes were under pressure to give up their land. In September 1830, members of the Choctaw tribe met with agents of the federal government. After a long and bitter argument, the Choctaw signed the Treaty of Dancing Rabbit. By signing, the Indians agreed to move to the newly formed Indian Territory, which is now the state of Oklahoma. About one hundred Choctaw families remained in Mississippi. They were each given 100 acres (40 ha) of land. Today, their descendants live near the town of Philadelphia on a small Choctaw reservation.

By 1832, most Native American land in Mississippi had been ceded to the United States. On October 20, 1832, the Chickasaw, under Chief Levi Colbert, signed the Treaty of Pontotoc Creek. The Indians turned over nearly 6 million acres (2 million ha) to the United States. The Chickasaw left their native lands in Mississippi and moved to the Indian Territory.

With statehood established and American Indian lands available for settlement, new settlers flooded into Mississippi. A booming population and the promise of cheap land lured people from other states and foreign countries to try farming the fertile soil. A Mississippi state official proclaimed, "Kentucky's coming, Tennessee's coming, Alabama's coming, and they're all coming to join the joyous crowd of Mississippians."

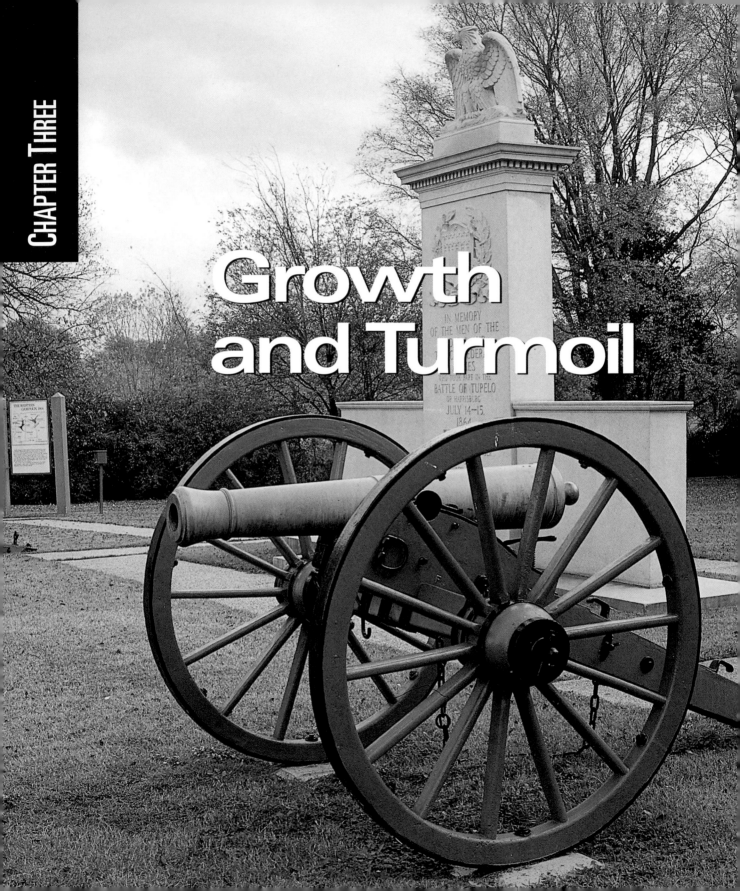

CHAPTER THREE

Growth
and Turmoil

Nothing in the history of the South is more spectacular than the rise of cotton as its principal crop. Cotton farming was not very profitable, however, until 1793—the year in which Eli Whitney invented the cotton gin (the word *gin* is short for *engine*). The machine separated the cotton seeds from the fibers ten times faster than they could be separated by hand. The faster processing meant that plantation owners could plant more acres and produce more cotton.

Landowners depended on slaves to harvest their cotton crops.

In 1806, a new variety of cottonseed, called Petit Gulf, was brought to the South from Mexico. This seed produced more cotton per plant, and further increased the crop yield. Before the invention of the cotton gin and the introduction of Petit Gulf, the South had raised 1.5 million pounds (675,000 kg) of cotton in one year. Only thirty years later, in 1820, it produced 160 million pounds (72 million kg).

The Cost of Cotton

King Cotton brought wealth to the South, but success came on the backs of slave laborers. As plantations raised more and more cotton, the need for cheap labor increased. Although the importation of slaves from foreign countries had been abolished in the United States in 1808, laborers were traded between the states. The South's slave population continued to grow.

Opposite: Battle of Tupelo Monument in Tupelo

Soon after Mississippi became a state in 1817, it became one of the wealthiest states in the Union—mainly because of cotton trade. As cotton-plantation owners became wealthier, they dominated state government. They built huge plantation homes, and an aristocracy developed that was similar to the one in Europe. Cotton brought economic prosperity to Mississippi, but slavery—and Southerners' belief in its importance to their way of life—almost destroyed the state.

The "Peculiar Institution"

Even though many Southerners were aware of the injustice and cruelty of slavery, they accepted it as a necessary part of their lives. They referred to slavery as "the peculiar institution" and could not imagine a society without it.

Most Southerners did not own slaves, however. In 1860, there were 791,305 people living in Mississippi. Of those, 30,943 owned slaves; 3,552 owned more than thirty slaves. Many small farmers could not afford slaves. Most Mississippians tilled their own small farms, produced their own lumber, or raised their own cattle. Unlike the rich plantation owners, these farmers typically lived in two-room log houses, cooked over open fires, and worked long, hard hours.

Rich slaveholders who owned more than one plantation often hired white overseers to make sure the work was done and to maintain discipline. Rules were strict for slaves, and punishment for breaking those rules was swift and harsh. Most plantation owners would not allow slaves to learn to read or write. They feared that the slaves, once they were educated, would revolt against them.

Debating States' Rights

Since 1800, representatives of slaveholding states and nonslaveholding states had been debating each other in Congress. Whenever a new state was admitted to the union, legislators argued about whether or not slavery would be allowed there. To maintain a balance of power, for every "free" state admitted, a "slave" state also had to be admitted.

Many Southerners also spoke out on the issue of states' rights. Since the ratification of the U.S. Constitution in 1783, states had argued about how much power the federal government should have. Each state, they felt, should have the right to decide for itself about issues such as slavery and taxation. Many Southerners disliked being forced to comply with the federal government's decisions.

In the early years of the nineteenth century, many Southerners became upset when Congress overruled their local policies. Even so, few Mississippians favored secession, or withdrawal from the union. Those feelings changed, however, as time passed. Through the 1850s, tempers flared again and again over what Mississippians felt was federal interference in their private decisions.

A heated argument in Congress over the slavery issue

Secession

Eventually, secession occupied every Southerner's mind. The "last straw" came when Abraham Lincoln won the 1860 presidential election. His Republican Party strongly opposed slavery, and many southern states had stated that they would leave the union if he were elected.

The break finally came. On January 9, 1861, Mississippi followed South Carolina to became the second state to secede from the Union. The vote in the Mississippi legislature was eighty-four to fifteen. The streets of Jackson erupted in celebration at the announcement of the vote. Bells rang and brass bands played as a glittering parade marched past the capitol. Newspaper headlines blared across the state, "Mississippi is out!"

A total of eleven states eventually left the union and formed their own government, the Confederate States of America (CSA). Mississippians' excitement about secession increased when they learned that their own former U.S. senator, Jefferson Davis, would become the president of the Confederacy.

Jefferson Davis

Jefferson Davis (1808–1889) was born in Christian County (later Todd County), Kentucky, but grew up in Wilkinson County, Mississippi. He graduated from the U.S. Military Academy and was a hero in the Mexican War (1846–1848). Davis served as President Franklin Pierce's secretary of war from 1853 to 1857. He also represented Mississippi as a U.S. congressman and senator.

When Lincoln became president in 1860, Davis resigned from the Senate and returned home. The Confederate convention, which met in Montgomery, Alabama, named him as provisional president of the Confederacy. He was inaugurated as its official president on February 22, 1862.

When the Civil War began, many Southerners welcomed the conflict, thinking the South would quickly defeat the North. Davis did not share their optimism, however. He warned that it would be a war "the like of which men have not seen." ∎

The War between the States

The fighting began when Confederate troops fired on Fort Sumter, in the harbor of Charleston, South Carolina, on April 12, 1861. During the first year of the Civil War, little fighting actually took place on Mississippi soil. Regiments of Mississippi soldiers joined other Confederate forces, however, to fight in battles outside the state.

The retreat of the Confederate troops at the Battle of Shiloh

The first battle on Mississippi soil was the Battle of Shiloh in April 1862. Union and Confederate forces fought along the Mississippi–Tennessee border for control of the railroad that ran through northeastern Mississippi. After the Confederate defeat, Union general Henry W. Halleck brought 100,000 troops against Corinth, a major rail center.

Throughout the rest of 1862, fierce fighting took place in the northern part of the state at Iuka, Booneville, Chickasaw Bayou, Tallahatchie Bridge, Coffeeville, and Holly Springs. The most important Civil War battle in Mississippi, however, was the Battle of Vicksburg in 1863.

The Siege of Vicksburg

Part of the Union plan to defeat the Confederacy involved taking control of the Mississippi River. The Union believed that by block-

The Union captured Vicksburg by blockading the harbor and controlling the Mississippi River.

ading the South's harbors and controlling the river, it would cripple the Confederacy and force it to surrender. Because of the city's strategic location, the capture of Vicksburg was essential to the plan's success.

In the winter of 1862–1863, Union general Ulysses S. Grant launched his attacks on Vicksburg. In mid-May 1863, after he had lost 4,000 men in two, unsuccessful, direct attacks, Grant began a siege on the city. Union forces surrounded Vicksburg and trapped the Confederate forces, under the command of General John C. Pemberton. From positions around the eastern perimeter of the city and from gunboats on the river, the Union Army fired on Vicksburg.

The Battle of Millikin's Bend

On New Year's Day 1863, thousands of slaves were freed by Abraham Lincoln's Emancipation Proclamation. More than 17,000 former slaves from Mississippi joined the Union army and fought bravely against the Confederacy and against their former masters.

In the Battle of Millikin's Bend, part of Grant's Vicksburg campaign, black Union soldiers fought the longest bayonet battle of the war. (A bayonet is a knifelike weapon that attaches to the barrel of a rifle for use in hand-to-hand combat.) More than 7,000 soldiers were killed or wounded. Their commander, General Dennis, reported, "It is impossible for men to show greater bravery than the Negro troops in that fight." ■

The Fall of Vicksburg

The siege of Vicksburg lasted forty-seven days. Despite the constant shelling, regular worship services were still held at the local churches. In her diary, Emma Balfour, a member of Christ Episcopal Church, wrote: "With the deep boom of cannon taking the place of organ notes, . . . Reverend W. W. Lord preached the Gospel of eternal peace to an assemblage of powder-grimed and often blood-stained soldiery at Christ's Church."

To escape the relentless shelling, many citizens took refuge underground. They dug caves into the hillsides. Some caves had only one or two rooms; others held as many as 200 people. To provide some comfort, the caves often had carpets, furnishings, books, candles, and flowers.

Food grew scarce for citizens and soldiers within the city. On June 4, all surplus provisions were seized and rationed equally to everyone. By June 20, a full day's food allotment was "two common biscuits, 2 rashers (slices) of bacon, a few peas and a spoonful of rice." Drinking water was also in short supply.

General John C. Pemberton surrendered Vicksburg to Grant's Union forces on July 4, 1863.

After suffering constant Union attack and now facing the prospect of widespread starvation, General Pemberton surrendered the city to Grant on July 4, 1863. When half-starved Confederate soldiers marched out to stack their rifles, cartridges, and flags, Grant's Union forces stood respectfully silent. Both sides remembered the heroism of the defenders of the city and the 40,000 Confederate and 10,000 Union soldiers who perished in the battle.

The End of the War

Despite its crippling losses, the bedraggled Confederate forces, the Army of the South, made a valiant effort to continue fighting the war. In the spring of 1865, however, the end came. On April 9, Confederate General Robert E. Lee surrendered to Union General Ulysses S. Grant in a solemn, dignified ceremony in the small town of Appomattox Courthouse, Virginia.

More than 3 million men fought in the Civil War. More than 600,000 died. Of the 78,000 soldiers from Mississippi who fought for the South, 36,000 lost their lives.

The Civil War had many names in Mississippi: The War of Northern Aggression, The War for Southern Independence, and The War between the States. Whatever it is called, the tragic four-year struggle freed the slaves, devastated the South, restored the Union, and forever changed the face of Mississippi.

The Civil War ended with Confederate general Robert E. Lee's surrender to Union general Ulysses S. Grant at Appomattox Courthouse in 1865.

A New State Constitution

The difficult years after the end of the Civil War, from 1865 to 1877, are called the period of Reconstruction. During this period, the federal government placed restrictions on the states in the former Confederacy to correct some of their prior injustices.

Immediately after the South's surrender, Mississippi's legislature passed the Black Codes. This legislation took away most of the civil rights that African-Americans had supposedly gained as a result of the Civil War. These laws excluded black Mississippians from serving on juries, voting, and holding public office. Mississippi refused to ratify the Thirteenth Amendment to the U.S. Constitution, which abolished slavery. It also refused to accept the Fourteenth Amendment, which granted citizenship to former slaves and guaranteed "equal protection of the laws" for all U.S. citizens.

Because of Mississippi's actions, Congress placed the state under military law. Andrew Johnson, who had become president after the death of Abraham Lincoln, appointed Lieutenant Colonel Adelbert Ames, a former Union general from Maine, as the Reconstruction governor of Mississippi. Under military rule, a state convention, including seventeen African-American delegates, set to work to draft a new state constitution.

The new Mississippi constitution was passed in December 1869, repealing the Black Codes and allowing black citizens the right to vote. Free public education was extended to all children, white and black, and racial discrimination was outlawed. With this new constitution, Mississippi was readmitted to the Union on February 23, 1870. Under the new government, black Mississip-

Reverend Hiram R. Revels

pians gained political power in the state. Thirty-six members of the 140-member state legislature were African-American. In 1870, Reverend Hiram R. Revels, a black minister from Natchez, became the first African-American to become a U.S. senator.

Scalawags and Carpetbaggers

Economic recovery after the war was slow for Mississippi. Damage to farms and industries and the loss of so many lives made recovery difficult. The emancipation of the South's slave labor force also contributed to Mississippi's economic woes. In addition, government corruption on both state and local levels sabotaged attempts at recovery.

During Reconstruction, many people tried to help African-Americans become involved in state government. Some were sincere, but others were motivated by greed. Two groups who were despised by white Southerners were the scalawags and the carpetbaggers.

Southerners originally used the term *scalawag* to refer to use-less cattle. During Reconstruction, the term was applied to Southerners who believed in the rights of African-Americans and worked with northern Republicans. Some Southerners believed that scalawags were traitors and called them "beasts in men's clothing."

Contrary to popular opinion, however, not all scalawags were worthless scoundrels. Most were Southern planters and business-men who had opposed secession. Many of them felt that the South had to change its social and racial views in order to survive. Their attempts at reform were largely unsuccessful, however, and they lost their leadership to a group of Northerners known as carpet-baggers.

Carpetbagger was a term scornfully used by Southerners to refer to a Northerner who moved to the South during Reconstruc-

Carpetbaggers came to the South during Reconstruction. Some had good intentions, but many did not.

tion. Southerners chose the name because most of these Northerners came with few possessions—just enough to fill a carpetbag, a cloth suitcase. Some Northerners—schoolteachers, for example—came to the South with good intentions. Most carpetbaggers, however, came with selfish goals, seeking to profit from the ravaged state or hoping to be elected to public office.

Members of the Ku Klux Klan wore sheets to shield their identities as they threatened and often killed African-Americans.

Dark Days

By 1875, white Mississippians, bitter about the Civil War and Reconstruction, regained political power in the state. They forced the Reconstruction governor to resign. White Democrats pushed through new state legislation that denied African-Americans many of their civil rights. They prevented blacks from voting through a campaign of threats, beatings, murders, and lynchings (illegal hangings).

The newly formed Ku Klux Klan, a secret society organized in the South, promoted white supremacy—the idea that whites are superior to all other races. Klan members beat and often killed African-Americans and any whites thought to be sympathetic to them.

Equal rights were denied to blacks, and the state passed a series of so-called Jim Crow laws to enforce strict segregation (separation) of the races. *Jim Crow* refers to a character in a southern song-and-dance routine that was popular in the 1820s and 1830s. The name became a derogatory term for a black person, implying inferior status.

In 1890, African-Americans in Mississippi suffered another setback. A constitutional convention, which had only one African-American delegate, drafted a new state constitution that stripped blacks of their civil rights. The convention imposed a literacy test, a complex set of residence requirements, and a poll tax—all designed to disqualify African-Americans from voting. The restrictions were so biased that even educated, middle-class blacks who had been state residents all their lives could not pass them. This policy of discrimination against black citizens continued in Mississippi well into the twentieth century.

A Speech to Heal a Nation

Lucius Quintus Cincinnatus Lamar (1825–1893) served in the U.S. House of Representatives from 1857 to 1860. In 1861, he drafted Mississippi's Ordinance of Secession, urging his fellow Mississippians to withdraw from the Union. After the defeat of the Confederacy, he returned to Washington and again served in the House and later in the Senate.

In 1874, Lamar delivered a moving speech to the members of Congress. He honored the late Senator Charles Sumner of Massachusetts, long hated by Southerners for his harsh policies toward the South.

Lamar pleaded with the nation for unity after the nightmares of the Civil War and Reconstruction. He said, "On both sides we must most earnestly desire to be one . . . in feeling and in heart. . . . My countrymen! Know one another and you will love one another."

Lamar's emotional plea captured the nation's attention and helped heal the relationship between North and South. In his book *Profiles In Courage,* President John F. Kennedy said of Lamar's address: "Few speeches in American political history have had such immediate impact." ■

After the Civil War, many freed slaves continued to work for landowners as tenant farmers or sharecroppers.

Century's End

From the end of Reconstruction in 1877 until the turn of the century, Mississippians endured financial hardship. Without slave labor, cotton farming became much less profitable for plantation owners.

The freed slaves worked as tenant farmers or sharecroppers. They would often farm a piece of the plantation land that belonged to their former master. As payment for the right to farm the land, they had to hand over a large share of the harvested crop to the landowner. Few former slaves had any money of their own, so they had to buy seeds, fertilizer, and other farming supplies on credit from the landowners. At the end of the harvest season, their share of the crop would barely pay their debt, so the landlords had to extend more credit. Their debt to the landowners kept the share-croppers tied to the land. In many ways, they were no better off than they had been as slaves.

CHAPTER FOUR

Meeting New Challenges

The twentieth century brought drastic social changes to the United States. Historians call the period at the beginning of the century, from about 1900 to 1917, the Progressive Era. During this time, journalists, such as Lincoln Steffens, Upton Sinclair, and Mississippi's Ida B. Wells, called for reforms in government and industry. Social reformers protested the use of child labor in the country's factories. Politicians throughout the country worked to increase education opportunities, improve conditions in the poor sections of cities, and promote citizen involvement in government. In Mississippi, however, the changes came slowly.

Ida B. Wells

Ida Bell Wells

The daughter of slaves, Ida Bell Wells (1862–1931) was born in Holly Springs. As a young woman, she taught in Memphis, Tennessee, and wrote for a local black newspaper, *Living War.* Wells eventually purchased an interest in the *Memphis Free Speech* and became its editor. Through her outspoken articles and editorials, she became a passionate voice of protest against unequal treatment of African-Americans.

Wells' writings angered some people. In 1892, an angry mob broke into her newspaper office and destroyed her printing presses. She moved to New York City and then to Chicago to continue her crusade.

In 1908, Wells was among sixty citizens who founded the National Association for the Advancement of Colored People (NAACP). This organization is dedicated to ending discrimination against African-Americans and other minority groups. ■

Opposite: Law enforcement and African-American protesters clashing in Jackson after a memorial march for Medgar Evers in June 1963

Partial Progress

For the most part, the social reform throughout the country neglected the problems of African-Americans. Although many northern politicians spoke out against racial injustice, they actually did little to ensure racial equality.

In Mississippi, "progressive" politicians spoke only for working-class whites and small farmers. Two of these politicians, who accomplished a great deal for white citizens but upheld racism, were James K. Vardaman and Theodore G. Bilbo. Vardaman was Mississippi's governor from 1904 to 1908. Bilbo served as governor from 1916 to 1920 and again from 1928 to 1932. Both men sought economic reforms for whites but supported strict racial segregation in public places and accommodations.

In 1917, the nation's attention turned from social reforms to international issues. War broke out in Europe in 1915. The United States tried to stay out of the conflict, until German submarines attacked U.S. ships and killed American citizens.

World War I

In 1917, the United States entered World War I, and 66,000 men and women from Mississippi answered the call to serve in the armed forces. Camp Shelby was built southeast of Hattiesburg to serve as a principal U.S. Army training facility. One of the first military flight schools in the nation, Payne Field, was established at West Point, Mississippi.

Hundreds of Mississippians died in the war, and the state had its share of heroes. The most decorated World War I soldier from Mississippi was Sergeant Henry J. Tudury of Bay Saint Louis. In

1919, General John J. Pershing, commander of the Allied Expeditionary Force in Europe, personally presented Tudury with the Distinguished Service Cross for bravery in battle.

U.S. involvement in World War I stimulated industry in the North. Factories needed to produce more ships, weapons, ammunition, and uniforms, so they needed more workers. Some northern businesses sent representatives to recruit black workers from the South. With a dream of decent jobs, houses with floors and windows, schools for their children, and an escape from constant insult and humiliation in the South, many black Mississippians migrated to northern cities.

Sergeant Henry J. Tudury was Mississippi's most decorated soldier during World War I.

The Not-So-Roaring Twenties

After the end of World War I, during the 1920s, much of the United States enjoyed a period of prosperity—the so-called Roaring Twenties. Mississippi, however, was still having hard times. Because of low prices for their products, many farmers could not pay their mortgages and had to move away or rent their farms from the banks. Because of the farmers' losses, many banks closed. Damages from natural disasters also kept Mississippi in poor economic condition throughout the decade.

On April 12, 1927, floodwaters from the Mississippi River drove 100,000 residents in the Delta (the region between the Mississippi and Yahoo Rivers) from their homes and killed hundreds. Several areas remained under water for twelve weeks. In some places, the river swelled to a width of 100 miles (160 km). The cost of damages to crops and property in the state exceeded $204 million.

In 1929, the state and the country were both dealt a serious

In 1936, Governor Hugh White worked to attract new industries to Mississippi.

blow. On October 24, now known as Black Thursday, the value of stocks fell drastically, and the Great Depression began. Individual investors lost huge sums of money. Hundreds of banks locked their doors, and people panicked. In those days, if a bank failed or closed, all the money that people had deposited in the bank would be lost. Many companies had to lay off workers or go out of business, which led to widespread unemployment. By 1933, 25 percent of American workers did not have jobs. In Mississippi, thousands left their farms, hoping to find jobs in northern cities.

Mississippi acted boldly to improve its economy. In 1936, Governor Hugh White introduced a program called Balance Agriculture with Industry (BAWI). This program was designed to attract new industries to the state. Funding from President Franklin D. Roosevelt's New Deal programs also helped Mississippi. These federal programs, created to solve some of the problems of the Great Depression, promoted the mechanization of farming and brought electricity to rural areas.

World War II

A second war in Europe brought great changes to the United States and to Mississippi. World War II began on September 1, 1939, when Germany invaded Poland. England and France declared war on Germany and on its allies, Italy and Japan.

Once again, the United States tried to remain neutral. Early on the morning of December 7, 1941, however, the situation changed. U.S. military forces at Pearl Harbor, Hawaii, were attacked by Japanese fighter planes. The next day, the United States declared war on Japan and its allies.

About 250,000 men and women from Mississippi entered military service during World War II (1941–1945). Although they continued to experience racial discrimination and segregation while enlisted, more than 85,000 black Mississippians served their country in the armed forces.

During World War II, pilots trained at the Keesler Air Force Base in Biloxi.

Camp Shelby, south of Hattiesburg, was reactivated to train U.S. soldiers, and Keesler Air Force Base was established in Biloxi to train pilots. The newly constructed Ingalls Shipyard, established at Pascagoula in 1938 under the BAWI plan, built naval vessels for the war effort.

Training camps in the state attracted defense contracts. Workers left farms to work in war industries or at military bases. Biloxi and Hattiesburg, which had military bases nearby, boomed. For the first time, the cities of Mississippi experienced rapid growth.

Mississippi's economy continued to grow after World War II. Land values increased along the Gulf Coast. The lumber industry expanded, and Mississippi's farmers began to grow new crops, such as soybeans, and raise poultry and catfish.

The black population in rural areas of Mississippi, however, still struggled with poverty, single-crop farming, and racism. The immigration to northern cities that had begun around 1915 continued. Between 1910 and 1980, Mississippi's African-American population dropped from 56 percent to 35 percent.

In Honor of Heroes

In front of the Old Courthouse Museum in Vicksburg stands a monument erected by Company B 106th Engineers Association, a World War II veterans' organization. The monument honors a unit of Vicksburg and Warren County soldiers who fought in World War II. The plaque reads: "We were that which others did not want to be. We went where others feared to go, and did what others failed to do. We were American Soldiers."

More soldiers from Mississippi than from any other state were awarded the Congressional Medal of Honor during the years of World War II. A total of 4,185 Mississippi servicemen and servicewomen died in the war. ■

The introduction of the mechanical cotton picker and other agricultural machines also contributed to the drop in the black population. Fewer laborers were needed in the fields. Black workers relocated to Detroit, St. Louis, Chicago, and other northern cities where industrial jobs were available. This migration of the South's workforce to the North was one of the largest population migrations in U.S. history.

Civil Rights

After World War II, new attitudes among blacks led to social and political movements across the South. Black soldiers returning from military service were no longer willing to endure quietly the humiliation of racial discrimination. They and others demanded what the U.S. Constitution grants to all citizens—equal rights under the law. The Jim Crow South had to change.

In 1954, the U.S. Supreme Court declared, in the lawsuit *Brown* v. *Board of Education of Topeka,* that segregation in public schools is unlawful. The South stubbornly refused to comply with the decision and responded with anger and violence. In Mississippi, citizens' councils were created by white communities throughout the state to ensure that racial separation would continue. Bus stations, rest rooms, parks, theaters, restaurants, and water fountains continued to be labeled "Whites Only" or "Coloreds Only." In 1956, Mississippi created the infamous Sovereignty Commission to spy on civil rights demonstrations and do whatever was necessary to "keep blacks in their place."

Despite intense opposition by whites, the Mississippi civil rights movement was the strongest in the South during the 1950s and 1960s. In the spring of 1961, busloads of Freedom Riders began arriving from all over

Segregation in Mississippi meant that African-Americans were kept separate from whites, even in waiting rooms.

Robert Parris Moses

Robert Parris Moses was born in Harlem in New York City. He abandoned his graduate studies at Harvard University and moved to Mississippi to work for civil rights. In 1961, he joined the Student Nonviolent Coordinating Committee (SNCC), a civil rights activist group. By 1964, he was head of the Mississippi Summer Project, a voter-registration program of the Council of Federated Organizations (COFO). That year was a presidential-election year, and the summer during which the voter-registration drive took place became known as Freedom Summer. ■

the country. These young people, black and white, came to protest the Jim Crow laws. When their buses stopped in the southern towns, the young people entered segregated waiting rooms and lunch counters and quietly asked to be served. Hundreds were arrested for violating segregation laws. As a result of these young people's courage and the publicity they received on national television, people across the country demanded the repeal of segregation laws.

A Jackson policeman arresting a Freedom Rider for "breach of peace" in 1961.

The Violent Sixties

In 1962, James Howard Meredith fought for his right to enroll at the University of Mississippi.

Three pivotal events in Mississippi shocked the nation in the mid-1960s. Each had lasting effects on the country's civil rights movement. In the fall of 1962, James Howard Meredith, accompanied by federal marshals, tried to enroll as the first black student at the University of Mississippi in Oxford. Governor Ross Barnett refused to let Meredith enter. Stirred by Barnett's refusal to obey federal court orders to let Meredith enroll, students at the university rioted. President John F. Kennedy sent thousands of troops to stop the riots and enforce the court orders. Two demonstrators were killed, and 375 people were injured. On October 1, 1962, Meredith was finally admitted to the all-white institution. Federal troops remained stationed on the campus until Meredith's graduation in 1963.

Fannie Lou Hamer

Born in Montgomery County, Fannie Lou Hamer (1917–1977) was one of the nation's most beloved civil rights leaders. In 1964, she and the Mississippi Freedom Democratic Party (MFDP) challenged the all-white Democratic Party for the right to represent Mississippi at the Democratic National Convention. Although the MFDP was not seated at the convention, its historic Mississippi Challenge helped increase black participation in politics in the United States.

During the convention, Hamer testified before a nationally televised committee meeting about her treatment in the Jim Crow South. Her emotional testimony brought tears to the eyes of politicians and gave television viewers a rare glimpse into the realities of life for blacks in Mississippi.

In later years, Hamer worked to bring the Head Start program to preschoolers and to improve low-income housing. At her funeral service, Andrew Young, then U.S. ambassador to the United Nations, praised her tireless efforts toward black voter registration, saying, "None of us would be where we are now had she not been there then." A biography of Fannie Lou Hamer, *This Little Light of Mine,* by Kay Mills, was published in 1994. ■

The second significant event took place just after midnight on June 12, 1963, in a residential neighborhood in Jackson. Civil rights leader Medgar Evers, the head of Mississippi's NAACP, was shot in the back. His killer, white supremacist Byron de la Beckwith, was tried twice and set free each time. Both of the all-white juries were deadlocked, and the judges declared mistrials. Thirty-four years later, in 1994, Beckwith was tried a third time. A racially mixed jury finally convicted Beckwith for Evers's murder.

The third important event was the murder of three young men. During the Freedom Summer of 1964, more than 1,000 volunteers

MISSING CALL FBI

THE FBI IS SEEKING INFORMATION CONCERNING THE DISAPPEARANCE AT PHILADELPHIA, MISSISSIPPI, OF THESE THREE INDIVIDUALS ON JUNE 21, 1964. EXTENSIVE INVESTIGATION IS BEING CONDUCTED TO LOCATE GOODMAN, CHANEY, AND SCHWERNER, WHO ARE DESCRIBED AS FOLLOWS:

	ANDREW GOODMAN	JAMES EARL CHANEY	MICHAEL HENRY SCHWERNER
RACE:	White	Negro	White
SEX:	Male	Male	Male
DOB:	November 23, 1943	May 30, 1943	November 6, 1939
POB:	New York City	Meridian, Mississippi	New York City
AGE:	20 years	21 years	24 years
HEIGHT:	5'10"	5'7"	5'9" to 5'10"
WEIGHT:	150 pounds	135 to 140 pounds	170 to 180 pounds
HAIR:	Dark brown; wavy	Black	Brown
EYES:	Brown	Brown	Light blue

During the Freedom Summer of 1964, these three young men were murdered by members of the Ku Klux Klan.

from throughout the country came to Mississippi to encourage blacks to register to vote. Among them were Michael Schwerner and Andrew Goodman, both from New York City. On June 21, the two men and James Chaney, a young black man from Meridian, drove into Neshoba County to investigate the burning of a black church. They were arrested and jailed in Philadelphia, Mississippi. They were released later that night, but never made it out of the county. A gang of twenty-one Ku Klux Klan members stopped the men's car, executed them, and buried them in an earthen dam. No criminal charges were ever filed against the murderers, but seven of them were later convicted of violating the murdered men's civil rights. None served more than six years in jail.

The Aftermath of Violence

By the end of the racially tense summer of 1964, Mississippi civil rights activists had suffered six murders, hundreds of beatings, thirty-five shootings, and sixty-eight bombings or burnings of churches, businesses, or homes. The White Knights of the Ku Klux Klan were responsible for most of the violence.

Many Mississippians felt ashamed and angry about what had happened in their state. Because of the violence, industries were reluctant to open factories there. Young people left the state, frustrated by its slow progress toward racial equality. Entertainers refused to perform to segregated audiences. The message was clear: Mississippi had to change or lose its chance for a prosperous future.

Voting Rights Act of 1965

The Voting Rights Act of 1965, signed into law by President Lyndon B. Johnson, helped transform the state of Mississippi. The act forced all southern states to allow open voter registration for blacks. Soon, the black vote became a deciding factor in many elections. Within the next three decades, blacks gained positions in state and local government, in corporations, and on school and university campuses throughout Mississippi. In 1989, Charles Evers, the brother of slain civil rights leader Medgar Evers, was elected mayor of Fayette, Mississippi. He was the first black mayor in the state since Reconstruction.

According to the 1990 census, 877,285 blacks lived in Mississippi, representing 36 percent of the population. By 1992, more than 716 African-American government officials had been elected, the highest number in any state. In 1993, nearly one-fourth of the seats in the state legislature were held by black citizens—again, the largest percentage in the nation.

A Brighter Future

Once the old ideas of white supremacy and racial segregation began to disappear in the late 1960s, Mississippi began to look toward the future. Citizens of all races began to work together to make the state into what some people call an "economic miracle."

Since 1990, hundreds of corporations have located in

Mississippi, expanding the state's horizons in new directions. High-tech industries and research centers have opened. Stennis Space Center in Hancock County trains astronauts and develops new equipment for the country's space program. With its long-distance telephone companies and electronic-pager companies, today Mississippi is a major telecommunications center for the South.

Tourism in Mississippi is also thriving. Gambling casinos along the Gulf Coast and on the Mississippi River bring visitors to the state, as do the many internationally acclaimed cultural events. Although it still has problems, Mississippi has blossomed. Like its state tree, the magnolia, Mississippi's deep roots are firmly planted in its native soil and its branches are reaching for the sky.

The Lady Luck Riverboat Casino in Natchez

CHAPTER FIVE

A Land of Plenty

A petrified forest in Flora, Mississippi

During the millions of years since the earth was formed, oceans have many times covered the land that is now Mississippi. Sea creatures left their shells behind, forming limestone, which helped plant life grow when the land was exposed to sunlight. The creatures' decayed bodies formed oil and gas deposits. The soil became rich with sandstone, ocher, clay, chalk, lignite, and other substances that today are among the natural resources of Mississippi.

At the end of the Ice Age, glaciers that covered much of North America melted and receded, producing enormous amounts of water. At one time, a huge bay, thousands of miles long and hundreds of miles wide, extended from the Gulf of Mexico to Minnesota. As the bay slowly shrank, the water formed a river that extended from the northern part of the continent to the gulf. Silt and sand deposited at the mouth of the river, creating rich land.

Opposite: A forest in Natchez Trace Parkway

Prehistoric Life

Animals of all sizes and types lived on the land that is now Mississippi. Fossil remains prove the existence of animals ranging in size from tiny shellfish to creatures as large as whales. These whalelike creatures, about 70 to 80 feet (21 to 24 m) in length, are known as zeuglodons. Each of their vertebrae measured up to 16 inches (41 cm) long.

Plants also flourished in the warm, temperate climate of Mississippi. Fossils of petrified trees dating as far back as 36 million years were found in Flora, Mississippi. Over the course of millions of years, trees and lush vegetation covered the landscape, creating the land that Mississippians love today.

The Lay of the Land

Mississippi measures 48,286 square miles (125,061 sq km). In area, it the thirty-second-largest state in the United States. Its greatest width, east to west, is 142 miles (228 km). From north to south, it measures 340 miles (547 km).

Alabama lies to the east, Tennessee to the north, and Arkansas and Louisiana to the west. The western border winds and twists along with the ever-changing Mississippi River. In fact, the western boundary of the state has changed often, as the Mississippi River, swollen by floodwaters, cut new pathways

Mississippi's topography

across the land. Before 1930, when a federal program was created to control the path and flow of the river, the Mississippi changed course often, making it dangerous to live on or near its banks.

To the south, Mississippi borders the southeast corner of Louisiana, but 44 miles (71 km) of the state's southern border runs along the Gulf of Mexico. This border lies at sea level—the lowest point in the state. The highest point, Woodall Mountain in the northeast corner of the state, rises 806 feet (246 m).

Two main land regions lie within the state: the Mississippi Alluvial Plain and the East Gulf Coastal Plain. Each region's soil, resources, and character are unique.

The Alluvial Plain

Thousands of years ago, the Ohio River flowed farther south than it does today, pouring into the Mississippi River near what is now Greenville. The Yazoo and other rivers also met near this point.

A farmer plowing cotton in the Mississippi Delta

During times of flood, the rivers carried tons of silt. When the floodwaters receded, they left behind deposits of rich, black soil. The soil is called alluvial, meaning that it came from rivers. Over centuries, these deposits formed the 35,000 square miles (90,600 sq km) of fertile lowlands that make up the Alluvial Plain of the Mississippi River.

Controlling the Mighty River

When the Mississippi River flooded in 1927, hundreds of people were killed and thousands of acres of farmland and timber were ruined. In 1928, Congress passed the Flood Control Act and instructed the U.S. Army Corps of Engineers to find a way to keep the river from flooding again. In the 1930s, the engineers came up with a plan.

The Mississippi never flows in a straight line. It meanders across the land, sometimes almost doubling back upon itself. To streamline its course to the Gulf of Mexico, the engineers shortened the river by cutting through the narrow necks of land between the long loops. The process created crescent-shaped "oxbow" lakes in various places along the Mississippi, aided navigation, and made it safer for people to live along the mighty river. The riverbed was also dredged, or scooped out, to make the river deeper, increasing the amount of water it could carry. ■

The Alluvial Plain blankets the entire western edge of the state of Mississippi. The southern part is known as the River Lowlands. This narrow strip of land edging the banks of the Mississippi River was once called the Natchez District, named for the region's largest city.

North of Vicksburg, the plain expands east from the Mississippi River to the Yazoo, Tallahatchie, and Coldwater Rivers. The region between the Mississippi and the Yazoo Rivers is called the Delta. Until the 1850s, the area was covered with tangled woods and swamps. Planters cleared the land for farming and drained much of the swampland.

The soil of the Mississippi Alluvial Plain is some of the richest farmland in the world and produces large crops of cotton and soybeans. The first European planters also prospered on the rich soil; the great plantation mansions they built there are still admired today.

A cypress swamp near Pearl River

In the mid-nineteenth century, settlers cleared and converted much of the Mississippi Valley wetlands into farmland. Today, only about 20 percent of the original forested wetlands remain, mostly in Louisiana, Arkansas, and Mississippi. Conservation has preserved these areas for the animals that live there.

The East Gulf Coastal Plain

The East Gulf Coastal Plain covers all of the state's land east of the Alluvial Plain. The Coastal Plain is a patchwork of lowlands, prairies, and hilly and pine-forested regions crisscrossed by streams and low ridges.

Loess soil (a fine, yellowish-brown soil) forms the hills—sometimes called the Cane, Bluff, or Loess Hills—that dominate the western part of the region. In the northeastern part of the state are the Tennessee River Hills, where Woodall Mountain rises above the rest. The Piney Woods, also called the Pine Hills, are located in the southeastern area of the Coastal Plain. These hills are covered with longleaf and slash-pine forests.

Wetlands

At one time, the Mississippi Valley contained the largest expanse of forested wetlands in the country. The Alluvial Plain was a network of swamps, bayous, and hardwood forests. Before federal flood-control efforts begun in the 1930s, these lands were regularly inundated by floodwaters from the Mississippi and its tributaries. ■

Although there are small prairies in central Mississippi, the state's main prairie is in the Coastal Plain. The Black Belt, or Black Prairie—named for its black soil—is a long, narrow finger of land extending through part of northeastern Mississippi. Corn, cotton, and hay thrive in the farmlands of the Black Belt and provide excellent grazing for livestock.

The Gulf Coast lies at the southern tip of the Coastal Plain. The coastline is somewhat protected from the open ocean by a string of offshore islands. The region's white sandy beaches and warm ocean breezes attract many tourists.

Coastline and Islands

Mississippi's coastline extends 44 miles (71 km) along the Gulf of Mexico. The state has a total shoreline of 359 miles (578 km), however, including those areas along its numerous bays and coves. Biloxi, Saint Louis, and Pascagoula are the largest bays in Mississippi. About 25 miles (40 km) of coastline at Bay Saint Louis, between Biloxi and Point Henderson, are protected by the nation's longest sea wall.

This beach in Biloxi is part of Mississippi's 44-mile (71-km) coastline.

Deer Island lies near the mouth of Biloxi Bay, among a chain of small islands situated just off the coast. Mississippi Sound separates Cat, Horn, East Ship, West Ship, and Petit Bois Islands from the mainland.

Wildlife

The abundant wildlife in Mississippi is due to the state's mild climate, rich soil, abundant water, and forest conservation. Deer, rabbits, squirrels, foxes, opossums, armadillos, raccoons, muskrats, and beavers are found in the state's lush forests. The buffaloes, bears, and otters that once made their home there are gone now, having been hunted for food and fur until the species disappeared. Conservation efforts helped to keep the deer from disappearing, too.

Swampy areas teem with water moccasins and alligators. Hundreds of species of birds, including doves, ducks, hawks, blue herons, pelicans, seagulls, and mockingbirds, also thrive in the warm climate.

Mississippi is world famous for its catfish. Other game fish that fill the state's rivers, streams, ponds, and lakes include bass, bream, and crappie. Saltwater fishers find plenty of crabs, shrimp, oysters, menhaden, mackerel, and speckled trout in the Gulf of Mexico.

The great egret is among the many species of birds that live in Mississippi's swamps.

Trees and Plants

More than half of Mississippi is forested. Forestry and logging are major contributors to the state's economy. When trees are cut, new saplings are planted to ensure a supply of wood products for the future.

Mississippi boasts many types of trees, including the majestic oak.

Pines of several varieties are among Mississippi's most common trees, but cottonwood, hickory, cedar, elm, yellow poplar, willow, cypress, and oak trees are also numerous. There are also pecan, sweet gum, bald cypress, and tupelo trees—and the beautiful magnolia, the state tree.

Magnolia blossoms, the state flower, bloom in Mississippi, along with azaleas, camellias, black-eyed Susans, crepe myrtles, dogwoods, redbuds, and violets. Pink and white Cherokee roses make a favorite Mississippi bouquet.

Rivers

The Mississippi River is the world's third-longest river (2,348 miles; 3,779 km). The Mississippi River Basin, the area drained by the river and its tributaries, encompasses one-third of the area of the United States.

The Mississippi became America's most important waterway after the invention of the steam engine in the early nineteenth century. Thousands of steamboats navigated up and down the mighty river. Major ports were established at Natchez, Vicksburg, and Greenville, bringing wealth from the cotton trade to the state.

Mississippi's western and north-central river basin drains into the Mississippi River. The rivers included in this basin are the Big Black, Yazoo, Coldwater, Sunflower, and Talla-hatchie. Rivers in the state's eastern basin drain into the Gulf of Mexico. They include the Pearl, Pascagoula, and Tombigbee. In addition to the natural rivers in eastern Mississippi, a man-made canal, the Tennessee-Tombigbee Waterway, connects the Tennessee River in the northeast corner of the state to the Tombigbee River near Columbus.

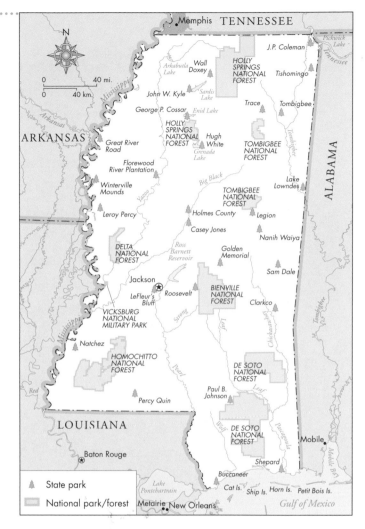

Mississippi's parks and forests

The Pascagoula River drains into the Gulf of Mexico.

A Land of Plenty **63**

Lakes and Bayous

Many of Mississippi's lakes are man-made reservoirs. In the northeast, the Tennessee River flows into Pickwick Lake. In north-central Mississippi are the Arkabutla, Enid, Grenada, and Sardis Reservoirs. Barnett Lake, a large reservoir built on the Pearl River in the early 1960s, is named after one-time Mississippi governor Ross Barnett. It provides water and recreation for the people of the nearby capital city of Jackson.

Along the Mississippi River, especially north of Vicksburg, are the oxbow lakes. These crescent-shaped lakes were formed when the government changed the course of the Mississippi River in the 1930s. Mississippi's oxbow lakes include Beulah, Lee, Moon, and Washington.

Mississippi also has many marshy, slow-moving streams called bayous, such as Bayou Pierre and Bayou Chitto. Some bayous connect lakes with the rivers in the Delta. Others link inland waterways with the Gulf of Mexico.

Mississippi's marshy, slow-moving streams are called bayous.

Climate

Mississippi has a moist, mild climate with short winters and long summers. Southern Mississippi boasts a frost-free season that lasts about 250 to 300 days each year. Farmers take full advantage of the long growing season.

Statewide, July temperatures average 81°F (27°C). In January, temperatures average 46°F (8°C). During the summer, temperatures remain fairly constant across the state. The temperature can seem much hotter, however, because of the high humidity.

Snow and sleet occasionally dust northern Mississippi, but the state's predominant form of precipitation is rain. Rainfall amounts range from 50 inches (127 cm) per year in the northwest to 65 inches (165 cm) in the more humid southeast.

Hurricanes

Throughout the state's history, hurricanes from the Gulf of Mexico have pounded the coast. On October 1, 1893, winds of 120 miles per hour (193 kph) struck the Gulf Coast, destroying everything in their path. An estimated 2,000 people in Mississippi, Louisiana, and Alabama died during that hurricane.

On June 27, 1957, Hurricane Audrey slammed into the coast of Louisiana, with 105 mile-per-hour (169 kph) winds and waves 20 feet (6 m) tall. Audrey did damage to several gulf states, killing 550 people in Louisiana, Mississippi, and Texas.

Tornadoes

Tornadoes have also caused extensive damage to Mississippi. On May 7, 1840, a tornado ripped through Natchez, sinking steam-

Crazy Kudzu

The kudzu vine was brought to the United States in 1876 from Japan and China as cattle feed and to control erosion—but it has caused more problems than it has solved. During the summer months, kudzu vines grow as much as 1 foot (30 cm) per day, covering trees, utility poles, and everything else nearby. Its common nicknames include Mile-a-Minute Vine, Foot-a-Night Vine, and The Vine That Ate the South. ■

Mississippi's Geographical Features

Total area; rank	48,286 square miles (125,061 sq km); 32nd
Land; rank	46,914 sq. mi. (121,507 sq km); 31st
Water; rank	1,372 sq. mi. (3,553 sq km); 22nd
Inland water; rank	781 sq. mi. (2,023 sq km); 27th
Coastal water; rank	591 sq. mi. (1,531 sq km); 10th
Geographic center	Leake, 9 miles (15 km) northwest of Carthage
Highest point	Woodall Mountain, 806 feet (246 m)
Lowest point	Sea level along the Gulf Coast
Largest city	Jackson
Longest river	Mississippi River
Population; rank	2,586,443 (1990 census); 31th
Record high temperature	115°F (46°C) at Holly Springs on July 29, 1930
Record low temperature	–19°F (–28°C) at Corinth on January 30, 1966
Average July temperature	81°F (27°C)
Average January temperature	46°F (8°C)
Annual precipitation	56 inches (142 cm)

boats on the river and destroying the ferry and sixty other flatboats. This violent storm killed 317 people, many of whom drowned in the Mississippi River.

In 1971, only two years after Hurricane Camille struck the Gulf Coast, several tornadoes ravaged Mississippi, claiming more than 100 lives and causing millions of dollars in damages. In 1996, for the second year in a row, the National Weather Service designated Mississippi the nation's most tornado-prone state.

Although it ranks fifth nationally in the annual number of tornadoes, Mississippi has had more tornado-related deaths than any other state: 1,182 since 1916. Sixty percent of all tornadoes in Mississippi are considered unusually "strong and violent," some having winds up to 300 miles per hour (483 kph).

Hurricane Camille

One of the most powerful hurricanes ever to hit the Mississippi coast came ashore on August 17, 1969. Hurricane Camille packed winds of up to 210 miles per hour (338 kph). The storm flipped automobiles, uprooted trees, and flattened crops. Huge waves crossed the coastal highway, destroying businesses and homes. The storm brought a surge of water 24 feet (7 m) high into Pass Christian. Waveland, Bay Saint Louis, Pass Christian, Long Beach, Gulfport, Biloxi, and Ocean Springs were heavily damaged by the storm. Ship Island, off the coast, was split by Camille into two islands, now called East Ship Island and West Ship Island. The open water between the islands has been named Camille Cut.

In two days, the hurricane killed 258 people in seven states, destroyed or damaged more than 45,000 homes, and caused approximately $1.5 billion in damages. ■

CHAPTER SIX

Touring Mississippi

No matter where you go in Mississippi, reminders of its historic past mingle with evidence of ongoing traditions, kept alive by people who love their state and want to keep its heritage alive. Every town has a story to tell, and every story involves people who love the land they call home.

Mississippians are fiercely loyal to their state, but a good-natured competition goes on among the residents of the five distinct regions. The people in the Delta, the Northeastern Hills, the Plains, the Heartland, and the Gulf Coast regions each prefer and praise the climate, history, and customs of their own area of the state.

The Mississippi Delta is an important part of the state's heritage.

The Delta

The Delta of Mississippi is sometimes called "the most southern place on Earth." The roots of its heritage come from the land. Cotton, catfish, and the music known as the blues are all from the Delta.

The blues began in the Delta cotton fields as slaves, then sharecroppers, sang to make their work go faster. The Delta Blues, a unique style of music reflecting the hardships of a working person's life, were influenced by West African tribal songs, slave work chants, and "hollers," the lonely, rambling, musical shouts that echoed through the cotton fields.

Opposite: Dunleith Plantation in Natchez

Clarksdale is the center of Mississippi's blues heritage. For decades, farmworkers from miles around have packed the streets of this northern Delta town on Saturday nights. They come to shop, to socialize, and to dance in the "juke joints" (clubs with jukeboxes). Dozens of these "joints" feature live performers on weekends. The Delta Blues Museum, established in 1979 in the city's public library, contains thousands of books, records, tapes, compact discs, and photographs documenting this unique style of music.

South of Clarksdale lies Greenville, the largest Mississippi city on the Mississippi River, with a population of 45,226. In May, the Mississippi Folklife Festival draws thousands of visitors to the city. The festival celebrates the rich cultural heritage of the Delta with gospel, blues, and jazz concerts, and crafts exhibitions and demonstrations.

In 1965, J. B. Williams dug the first catfish pond in Mississippi. Today, the area around Belzoni in Humphreys County is the world's leader in the production of farm-raised catfish. Each April, Bel-

Muddy Waters

Bluesmen Robert Johnson, Howlin' Wolf, John Lee Hooker, and W. C. Handy—the Father of the Blues—all lived in Clarksdale. The town is best known, however, as the hometown of the legendary Muddy Waters. McKinley Morganfield (1915–1983) carried the emotional, powerful Delta sound to Chicago, plugged it in, turned it up, and became famous as Muddy Waters.

Known as the Father of Electric Blues, he earned six Grammy awards and had his portrait on a U.S. postal stamp commemorating "Legends of Blues and Jazz." His music influenced musicians such as Elvis Presley, country music legend Jimmie Rodgers, and the Rolling Stones. Muddy Waters was inducted into the Rock and Roll Hall of Fame in 1986. ■

Jim Henson

Jim Henson (1936–1990) was born in Greenville and spent his early years in the nearby town of Leland. As a boy, Henson spent hours along Deer Creek, near his grandmother's home. The creek stimulated his imagination and gave birth to his idea for Kermit the Frog. Kermit, the world's most famous puppet, was named in honor of Henson's childhood friend Kermit Scott.

Henson's creations, the Muppets, are loved by children of all ages all over the world. Henson's career began with a Saturday-morning children's television show in Washington, D.C., and included *Sesame Street, Fraggle Rock, Muppet Babies, The Storyteller,* and five full-length movies. Henson died suddenly on May 16, 1990, but the characters he created will live forever. Deer Creek still runs through Leland, and the Jim Henson museum stands on its banks. ■

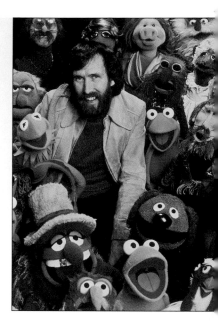

zoni's population of 2,536 swells to more than 20,000 as visitors arrive for the World Catfish Festival. Catfish lovers feast their eyes, ears, and appetites on arts and crafts exhibits, live music, and the "World's Largest Fish Fry." They compete in the Catfish Eating Contest and watch local beauties compete for the title of Catfish Queen. Belzoni's museum, the Catfish Capitol, features a 40-foot (12-m) statue of King Cat and a videotape presentation of the complete story of the catfish—from fingerling (a baby catfish) to the frying pan.

Farther south in the Delta is Yazoo City, made famous by the down-home stories of country humorist, Jerry Clower. Growing up in rural Mississippi

Mississippi is famous for its production of farm-raised catfish.

provided Clower with a wealth of local folklore and an endless supply of colorful characters to weave into his stories. The Pulitzer Prize–winning novelist Willie Morris, also a Yazoo City native, featured the local legend of the witch of Yazoo in his 1972 novel *Good Old Boy.* The witch was blamed for causing the fire that destroyed the town's central business district in 1904.

The Northeastern Hills

The Northeastern Hills of Mississippi feature rolling hills and lakes that once were home to the Chickasaw Nation. After the tribe was stripped of its lands in the 1832 Treaty of Pontotoc, speculators and surveyors divided the area into counties, towns, and farms.

During the Civil War, Union general Ulysses S. Grant made Holly Springs the major supply base for his first campaign against Vicksburg. The town retains a wealth of Civil War history and numerous antebellum ("before the war") mansions. Hillcrest Cemetery provides a resting place for thirteen Confederate generals and for citizens of Holly Springs who died during a yellow-fever epidemic in 1878.

East of Holly Springs is the small town of Ripley, incorporated as the county seat of Tippah County in 1837. Ripley is named for General Eleazor Wheelock Ripley, a hero of the War of 1812 and recipient of the Congressional Medal of Honor. Another of Ripley's famous citizens was Colonel William Clark Falkner, who served with the Confederate Army during the Civil War. During his life, Falkner wrote several novels. He was the great-grandfather of the famous American author William Faulkner (the letter *u* was later added to the name), who spent part of his childhood in Ripley.

Rowan Oak, novelist William Faulkner's home

Corinth, in the northeastern corner of Mississippi, is located at the junction of two important southern railroads: the Memphis & Charleston and the Mobile & Ohio. Corinth was an important transit point for Confederate troops and supplies during the Civil War. It was the site of more military action than any other town in the western Confederacy. Many of the houses commandeered by Union forces or occupied by Confederates still line the streets. Men who died in the Battle of Corinth in 1862 are buried in the national cemetery there.

Oxford was the hometown of William Faulkner, winner of Pulitzer and Nobel Prizes. Rowan Oak, the home where he wrote several of his works, is registered as a national historic landmark and is maintained as a museum by the University of Mississippi. The wooded campus of the university, which is known as Ole Miss, has three museums and an art gallery. The Center for the Study of Southern Culture displays exhibits on southern music, folklore, and literature. It also houses the University of Mississippi

Elvis Presley's birth-place in Tupelo

Blues Archives, which contains the personal music collection of blues legend B. B. King.

The largest city in the Northeast Hills is Tupelo, named for the Chickasaw phrase *tuh pu lah,* which means "to scream and make a noise." A federal fish hatchery at Tupelo, one of the oldest in the nation, sends about 3 million fish every year to farm ponds and reservoirs in thirty-eight northern Mississippi counties. Tupelo is most famous as the birthplace of Elvis Presley, the King of Rock and Roll. The house where he was born and lived as a child is open to the public. During his early years of fame, Elvis kept in touch with his Mississippi roots and came back from Memphis, Tennessee, to perform in Tupelo. The proceeds from a 1957 concert were donated to the city for the development of Elvis Presley Park.

The Plains

The Plains cover the eastern half of the state from the Northeast Hills to the Gulf Coast. Starkville, with a population of 18,458, was founded in 1831. It was originally called Boardtown, because a nearby mill provided the clapboard to construct the town's buildings. It was renamed in 1837 in honor of General John Stark, a hero of the American Revolution.

Just east of Starkville is the small town of Mississippi State, the home of Mississippi State University (MSU). MSU is the state's largest university and has more than 14,000 students. The university houses the Cobb Institute of Archaeology, which contains artifacts from American Indian mounds in the southeastern United States. Near Starkville are lakes and the Tennessee-Tombigbee Waterway for fishing, deep forest lands for hunting, trails for hiking or jogging, and championship golf courses.

Columbus lies east of Starkville on the Tombigbee River. Hernando de Soto, the first European explorer to visit the lands of Mississippi, arrived somewhere near this city's present-day location in 1540. The first trading post in the area was built there in 1784 by William Cooper, and the town was established in 1821. It was originally called Possum Town because of the opossumlike features of local trader Spirus Roach. When the city of Jackson fell to Union forces in 1863, Columbus served as the temporary state capital. The state's first free public school, Franklin Academy, was opened in Columbus in 1821. The nation's first institution for higher learning for women, now Mississippi University for Women, was established here in 1884.

Philadelphia, in the central part of the state, hosts the week-long Neshoba County Fair. *National Geographic* magazine called the fair "Mississippi's grand reunion." This campground fair is held the first week in August every year. State and national politicians make speeches while visitors gather in cabins to eat southern food, share stories, and recall fond memories of past fairs. Carnival rides, harness racing, and games of chance add to the festivities.

The Choctaw Indian Reservation, northwest of Philadelphia, is home to about 5,000 Choctaws. In mid-July each year, they hold the Choctaw Indian Fair. Members of the tribe perform native

The First Memorial Day

The first Memorial Day observation was held in Columbus in April 1863. The women of the city gathered at Friendship Cemetery and placed flowers on the graves of Confederate and Union soldiers buried there. The city's first formal observance of what was then known as Decoration Day was on April 25, 1866. National observance began on May 30, 1868. Today, the holiday falls on the last Monday in May each year. Modern Memorial Day celebrations, honoring all soldiers who have died serving their country, include military parades, patriotic speeches, and the sale of small, red, artificial poppies to benefit disabled veterans. ■

The Choctaw Indians hold fairs that include dancing and games.

dances and play the traditional game of stickball. The Choctaw Museum of Southern Indians exhibits artifacts and tells the history of the Choctaw people and other southern tribes. Northeast of the reservation is the Nanih Waiya Historic Site. This mound, according to legend, is the birthplace of the Choctaw.

Southeast of Philadelphia, the town of Meridian is the site of the Jimmie Rodgers Museum, housed in an old railroad depot. Rodgers, America's first folk singer, was known as the Father of Country Music. He once worked for the railroad and was also called the Singing Brakeman. After his death in 1933, Rodgers was the first country-music artist inducted into the Country Music Hall of Fame.

Founded in 1882, Hattiesburg is the largest city in the southern Plains, with a population of 41,882. The city, named for Hattie Hardy, the wife of founder Captain William H. Hardy, is home to the University of Southern Mississippi. Situated at the edge of the De Soto National Forest, the city is the center for the lumber industry in southeastern Mississippi. Hattiesburg is known as the Hub City. Major highways—from Alabama, Louisiana, and the Mississippi Gulf Coast—converge there like the spokes of a wheel. Every year, thousands of people attend the Old Time Festival and HUBfest. The historic Camp Shelby, just south of town—which served as a training facility, prisoner-of-war camp, and troop-staging area during the First and Second World Wars—is today the largest, permanent National Guard Field Training Site in the country.

The Heartland

Jackson, Mississippi's capital and the largest city in the state, is home to nearly 200,000 people. The city is impressively situated on the bluffs of the Pearl River. Its center is laid out in a checkerboard pattern suggested by Thomas Jefferson. Jackson began as a French trading post called Le Fleur's Bluff in 1792. It was chosen as the state capital in 1821. The city was named for Major General Andrew Jackson, hero of the Battle of New Orleans in the War of 1812 and the seventh president of the United States. During the Civil War, Jackson was invaded four times by Union forces. General Sherman, under orders from General Grant, burned the city in 1863. The city earned the nickname Chimney-ville for what remained of the city.

Gardens at the University of Southern Mississippi in Hattiesburg

Jackson is very much the heart of Mississippi—the center of arts, government, commerce, and manufacturing. It is a sprawling, friendly city with a small-town quality. In 1965, the first Mississippi Arts Festival was held in Jackson. The four-day event featured internationally known artists, such as pianist Van Cliburn. The festival was so successful, with more than 75,000 attending, that

Jackson is the state's capital and its largest city.

Jackson now hosts it annually. Every year, the city also hosts the Dixie National Rodeo—the largest such event east of the Mississippi River, sponsored by the Professional Rodeo Cowboys Association.

West of Jackson is Vicksburg, best known for its importance during the Civil War. In 1863, Union general Ulysses S. Grant laid siege to the city for forty-seven days. The Vicksburg National Military Park, said to be the best-preserved Civil War battlefield in the nation, commemorates this incredible battle. The park also displays the partially restored Union gunboat USS *Cairo* (pronounced "kay-row"), sunk by Confederates in the Yazoo River near Vicksburg in 1862. Encased in mud for more than 100 years, the *Cairo* was raised in 1964 and placed on display in a special pavilion. An adjacent museum houses hundreds of perfectly preserved Civil War artifacts brought up with the ship.

Historic Natchez, farther south on the banks of the Mississippi River, is one of the oldest cities in North America. Evidence of its earliest inhabitants can be found near the banks of Saint Catherine Creek. From 1200 to 1729, Natchez Indians occupied the area known today as the Grand Village of the Natchez. The French came to the area in 1716 and built Fort Rosalie on a bluff overlooking the Mississippi River. A settlement near the fort took the name of the tribe living nearby—Natchez. Today, Grand Village is a national historic landmark located within the city, with a museum and educational programs for school and adult groups.

Natchez, one of the oldest cities in North America, is known for its historical homes and tours.

The steamboat era began when the first steamboat, the *New Orleans,* docked in Natchez in 1811. From 1820 to 1860, the cotton trade brought great prosperity to the port city. Because it was not of strategic military importance, Natchez escaped heavy damage during the Civil War. As a result, more than 500 antebellum structures still stand today. Every spring, Natchez hosts a tour of thirty-two of its historic homes built by wealthy citizens. Mansions such as Melrose, Stanton Hall, and Longwood are open to visitors who are greeted by ladies in Civil War–era costumes.

One of the most famous pathways in the country, the Natchez Trace, begins just outside Natchez and extends northeastward across the state into Nashville, Tennessee. The route has been used for centuries—by Native Americans, European trappers, river boatmen returning home, frontier settlers, and slave traders. In

Natchez Mansions

Melrose was built by John R. McMurran, a prominent lawyer and planter, from 1841 to 1845. Its 84 acres (34 ha) is thick with azaleas, dogwoods, redbuds, cypresses, magnolias, and live oaks. Many of the original furnishings are still in the house, including whale-oil chandeliers and a rare piano.

Stanton Hall (above) is one of the most visited national historic landmarks in the United States.

Built in 1857 by Frederick Stanton, its grounds occupy an entire city block. No expense was spared in constructing or furnishing the house. The mansion is covered in white stucco, and Corinthian columns stand on the front porch. Every room has a bronze chandelier. Silver doorknobs and hinges from England, gold-leaf mirrors from France, and white marble mantels from New York fill the house.

Longwood today stands unfinished among trees draped with Spanish moss. Dr. Haller Nutt, a cotton planter, wanted the house to be unique—from its octagon shape to the onion-shaped dome crowning a sixteen-sided observation tower on its roof. Work stopped after two years, in 1861, when the Civil War began. Only nine of the thirty-two rooms were completed. ◾

1938, the National Park Service began constructing a modern parkway that closely follows the course of the original Natchez Trace. Today, the Natchez Trace Parkway, a 444-mile (715-km) highway, stretches diagonally across Mississippi.

The Gulf Coast

The Mississippi Gulf Coast region offers visitors and residents sandy beaches, warm breezes, fishing, swimming, and boating. Floating casinos, the state's newest sources of revenue, dot the coastline.

The largest and oldest of Mississippi's coastal cities is Biloxi, originally settled in 1699. The city's name comes from the Biloxi Indians and means "broken pot." Because its 300-year history is visible everywhere, visitors call Biloxi "a museum without walls." Since 1840, the city has been a popular, coastal resort. Freshwater, saltwater, and deep-sea fishing attract anglers year-round. Crepe myrtles, roses, camellias, and magnolias flourish in the warm, moist climate, and oaks draped with lacy shawls of Spanish moss line the streets. After Hurricane Camille ravaged the Gulf Coast in 1969, rebuilding efforts included the construction

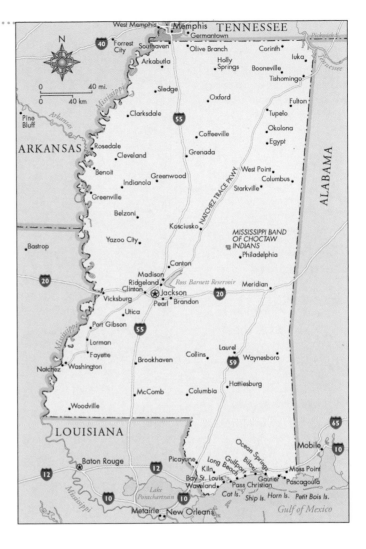

Mississippi's cities and interstates

The Mississippi Gulf Coast provides fishing, swimming, and boating for its visitors.

The Old Biloxi Lighthouse

The Old Biloxi Lighthouse, built in 1848, is one of the city's most famous structures. During the Civil War, the 65-foot (20-m) cast-iron tower was threatened by a Union invasion. Someone climbed to the top of the lighthouse, removed the lens from the light, and buried it for safekeeping.

In 1865, Mississippians who mourned the death of Abraham Lincoln painted the lighthouse black. Today, the Old Biloxi Lighthouse, repainted white, stands in the middle of a four-lane highway. ■

of the Harrison County Sand Beach. The man-made strip of white sand stretches 26 miles (42 km) along the Gulf Coast, the world's longest artificially created beach.

Pascagoula is the home of one of the nation's great shipbuilding centers: Ingall's Shipyard, a division of Litton Industries. Ingall's employs about 10,000 workers who have built some of the U.S. Navy's most sophisticated ships. The state's oldest building, the Old Spanish Fort, is also located in Pascagoula. Built in 1718, its massive 18-inch (45-cm) walls are made of heavy timbers and cemented with oyster shells.

Near the town of Bay Saint Louis, at the west end of the Gulf Coast, is the John C. Stennis Space Center, named for Senator John C. Stennis (1901–1991), who represented Mississippi from 1947 until his retirement in 1988. The site in Hancock County was selected by the National Aeronautics and Space Administration

The John C. Stennis
Space Center in
Hancock County

(NASA) in October 1961 as the nation's first test facility for the *Saturn V* rocket program. In 1969, Neil Armstrong traveled to the moon in a space vehicle tested at the Stennis Space Center. The first test firing of a space shuttle's main engine was conducted at the center in June 1975.

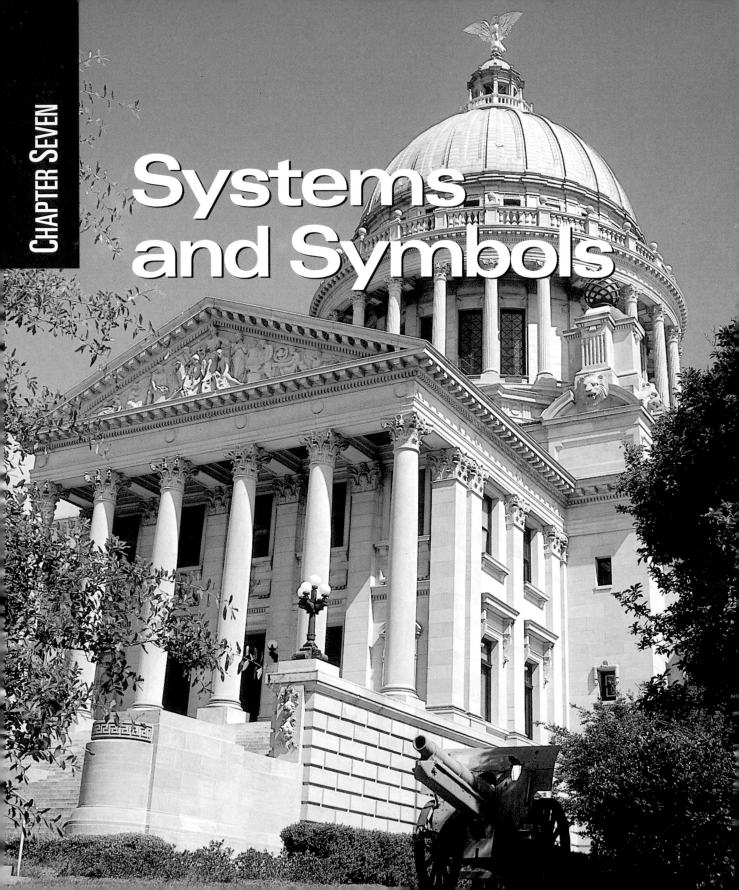

CHAPTER SEVEN

Systems and Symbols

n his second inaugural address in 1996, Mississippi Governor Kirk Fordice—the first Republican governor of the state since Reconstruction—said, "The best is yet to be in Mississippi. . . . We are a people of vision, optimism, imagination, and possess a fighting spirit that refuses to be broken." Mississippi's constitution, state and local governments, and state symbols all demonstrate the great pride—and unity—of its people.

For much of the state's history, a large percentage of the people were kept out of government, but since the Voting Rights Act of 1965, everything has changed. Today, Mississippi's state government is truly "of the people, and by the people." All races share political power and work together for the future of the state.

Governor Kirk Fordice brought optimism and growth to his state.

The Constitution

The state had three previous constitutions—adopted in 1817, 1832, and 1869. Its present constitution was adopted in 1890. Amendments, or changes, to the constitution may be proposed by a two-thirds majority of the state legislature. Before a proposed amendment becomes law, it must be approved by a majority of voters in a general election. The constitution can also be amended by a constitutional convention called by a majority of the members of each house of the state legislature.

Opposite: The capitol in Jackson

The structure of Mississippi's state government is similar to the structure of the federal government in Washington, D.C. Each of its three branches—executive, legislative, and judicial—has specific powers and responsibilities. The branches act as a check on one another, so a balance of power is maintained.

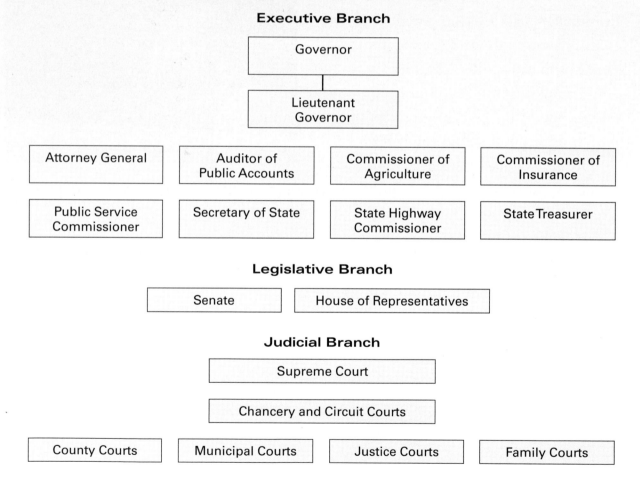

Mississippi's State Government

Executive Branch

Governor

Lieutenant Governor

Attorney General	Auditor of Public Accounts	Commissioner of Agriculture	Commissioner of Insurance
Public Service Commissioner	Secretary of State	State Highway Commissioner	State Treasurer

Legislative Branch

Senate   House of Representatives

Judicial Branch

Supreme Court

Chancery and Circuit Courts

County Courts   Municipal Courts   Justice Courts   Family Courts

Mississippi's Governors

Name	Party	Term	Name	Party	Term
David Holmes	Dem.-Rep.	1817–1820	John M. Stone	Dem.	1876–1882
George Poindexter	Dem.-Rep.	1820–1822	Robert Lowry	Dem.	1882–1890
Walter Leake	Dem.-Rep.	1822–1825	John M. Stone	Dem.	1890–1896
Gerard C. Brandon	Dem.-Rep.	1825–1826	Anselm J. McLaurin	Dem.	1896–1900
David Holmes	Dem.-Rep.	1826	Andrew H. Longino	Dem.	1900–1904
Gerard C. Brandon	Dem.-Rep.	1826–1832	James K. Vardaman	Dem.	1904–1908
Abram M. Scott	Dem.	1832–1833	Edmond F. Noel	Dem.	1908–1912
Charles Lynch	Dem.	1833	Earl L. Brewer	Dem.	1912–1916
Hiram G. Runnels	Dem.	1833–1835	Theodore G. Bilbo	Dem.	1916–1920
John A. Quitman	Whig	1835–1836	Lee M. Russell	Dem.	1920–1924
Charles Lynch	Dem.	1836–1838	Henry L. Whitfield	Dem.	1924–1927
Alexander G. McNutt	Dem.	1838–1842	Dennis Murphree	Dem.	1927–1928
Tilghman M. Tucker	Dem.	1842–1844	Theodore G. Bilbo	Dem.	1928–1932
Albert G. Brown	Dem.	1844–1848	Martin Sennett Conner	Dem.	1932–1936
Joseph W. Matthews	Dem.	1848–1850	Hugh L. White	Dem.	1936–1940
John A. Quitman	Dem.	1850–1851	Paul B. Johnson	Dem.	1940–1943
John I. Guion	Dem.	1851	Dennis Murphree	Dem.	1943–1944
James Whitfield	Dem.	1851–1852	Thomas L. Bailey	Dem.	1944–1946
Henry S. Foote	Union Dem.	1852–1854	Fielding L. Wright	Dem.	1946–1952
John J. Pettus	Dem.	1854	Hugh L. White	Dem.	1952–1956
John J. McRae	Dem.	1854–1857	James P. Coleman	Dem.	1956–1960
William McWillie	Dem.	1857–1859	Ross R. Barnett	Dem.	1960–1964
John J. Pettus	Dem.	1859–1863	Paul B. Johnson	Dem.	1964–1968
Charles Clark	Dem.	1863–1865	John Bell Williams	Dem.	1968–1972
William L. Sharkey	Whig-Dem.	1865	William Waller	Dem.	1972–1976
Benjamin G. Humphreys	Whig	1865–1868	Cliff Finch	Dem.	1976–1980
Adelbert Ames	U.S. Military Gov.	1868–1870	William F. Winter	Dem.	1980–1984
			William A. Allain	Dem.	1984–1988
James L. Alcorn	Rep.	1870–1871	Ray Mabus Jr.	Dem.	1988–1992
Ridgley C. Powers	Rep.	1871–1874	Kirk Fordice	Rep.	1992–
Adelbert Ames	Rep.	1874–1876			

The governor lives in a mansion that was modeled after the White House in Washington, D.C.

The Executive Branch

The executive branch enforces laws and administers the state's business. Voters elect a governor to head the executive branch. The governor serves a four-year term and may serve two consecutive terms. He approves or vetoes laws passed by the legislature and can call special sessions, if needed, to handle specific problems.

Voters also elect other members of the executive branch. The lieutenant governor is second in command. He serves as president of the senate, but only votes to break a tie. The secretary of state monitors elections and keeps records of official government acts. The attorney general is the top legal official and makes sure that the state's laws are enforced.

The auditor of public accounts and the treasurer take care of Mississippi's finances. Other members of the executive branch head state agencies and advise the governor. They are the commissioner of agriculture, the state highway commissioner, the public service commissioner, and the commissioner of insurance. All of these officials serve four-year terms.

The Legislative Branch

The legislative branch makes Mississippi's laws. Modeled after the U.S. Congress, this branch consists of a state legislature with two separate houses, or chambers. The senate has 52 members and the House of Representatives has 122 members. All legislators are elected to four-year terms. Every two years, half the legislators are eligible for reelection.

Senators and representatives meet for ninety days each year, except in the first year after a gubernatorial (governor's) election. In those years, the legislative session lasts 125 days. Regular legislative sessions begin each year on the Tuesday after the first Monday in January.

Besides proposing and passing laws, the legislature also proposes amendments to the state constitution. If necessary, the legislature can override the governor's veto of new laws with a two-thirds majority of both houses.

The interior of the Mississippi Senate chambers

The Judicial Branch

The judicial branch interprets laws passed by the legislature. Mississippi's highest court is the state supreme court. Voters elect nine justices to serve eight-year terms. The justice who has served the longest acts as chief justice of the supreme court.

The main trial courts in Mississippi are the chancery courts and the circuit courts, which have a total of seventy-nine judges. Chancery court judges hear civil cases, which involve non-criminal disputes between individuals. Circuit court judges hear both criminal and civil cases.

Other courts in the state include county, municipal, justice, and family courts. All judges in these courts serve four-year terms.

Local Government

The county is the chief unit of local government in Mississippi. There are eighty-two counties in the state. Each county is administered by

Mississippi's counties

a board of supervisors having five elected members. The state has approximately 500 cities and towns, but only 294 of them have organized city governments. Most of the 294 are governed by a mayor and a town council.

National Politics

The Democratic Party has dominated Mississippi's politics throughout most of the state's history. In every presidential election from 1876 through 1944, Mississippi cast its electoral votes for the Democratic candidate. Third-party candidates were successful, however, in 1948, 1960, and 1968, when racial issues were predominant. In those years, Independent candidates, usually southerners who shared Mississippi's opinion on race relations, carried the state. Since 1968, the state has usually voted for the Republican candidate.

Mississippi voters elect two U.S. senators and five U.S. representatives. U.S. senators serve six-year terms, and U.S. representatives serve two-year terms.

The Capitol and Governor's Mansion

The state capitol in Jackson was built in 1903 at a cost of $1,093,641. It was designed by renowned architect Theodore C.

Link of St. Louis, Missouri, and constructed on the site of an old state penitentiary. In the center of the building, a huge dome rises 180 feet (55 m) above ground level. An 8-foot (2.4-m) tall, gold-leafed copper eagle with a wingspan of 15 feet (4.5 m) perches atop the dome.

The Old Capitol was built in 1903.

The Old Capitol was the state's capitol from 1839 to 1903. The state's secession convention was held there in 1861, when Mississippi became the second state to secede from the Union. The building was restored from 1959 to 1961 at a cost of approximately $2 million. Today, it houses the Mississippi State Historical Museum.

Near the Old Capitol is the governor's mansion, the official home of Mississippi's governor and his family since its completion in 1841. Modeled after the White House in Washington, D.C., the mansion also served as Union General William Tecumseh Sherman's headquarters during his occupation of Jackson in 1863.

The State Flag and Seal

On February 7, 1894, the state legislature appointed a committee to design the flag of Mississippi. The "stars and bars" in the upper left corner is a replica of the Confederate army battle flag, used during the Civil War. It represents the state's membership in the Confederacy. The remainder of the flag is made up of three horizontal bars, in the national colors of red, white, and blue.

Adopted in 1817, the state seal features an eagle with outstretched wings. On its breast is a shield with vertical stripes below a field of thirteen stars. In its talons, the eagle holds a bundle of arrows and a palm branch. Below the eagle is a single, five-pointed star. Within the double border around the eagle are the words "The Great Seal of the State of Mississippi." ■

Mississippi's State Symbols

State flower: Magnolia blossom The magnolia's sweet-smelling blossoms (left) and deep green leaves grace many southern gardens. In 1900, the children of Mississippi chose the magnolia as the state flower. It was officially designated by the 1952 legislature.

State tree: Magnolia Designated as the state tree on April 1, 1938, the magnolia has large, dark green, leathery leaves and bears snowy-white, fragrant flowers and conelike fruits. It grows very slowly and can reach heights of 100 feet (30 m). Mississippi is the only state to have the state tree's blossom as the state flower.

State land mammal: White-tailed deer White-tailed deer, also called Virginia deer, are the most common large game animals in North America. They may stand 3 1/2 feet (1 m) tall and weigh 200 pounds (91 kg). Their tails, for which they are named, grow about 1 foot (30 cm) long. When the deer are frightened and begin to run, the tails stand straight up, showing the white underside.

State water mammal: Bottle-nosed dolphin Star performers in many aquariums and theme parks, these dolphins delight audiences with their tricks. Along the coast of Mississippi, bottle-nosed dolphins frolic beside ships entering and leaving port.

State bird: Mockingbird Found throughout Mississippi, mockingbirds (bottom, left) are named for their ability to copy the songs of other birds. Many children enjoy whistling to a mockingbird and listening as it tries to imitate the tune. The mockingbird was selected as the state bird by the Women's Federated Club and the state legislature in 1944.

State waterfowl: Wood duck Wood ducks are colorful birds that live on the lakes and ponds of Mississippi. They are usually about 20 inches (51 cm) long. The legislature designated the wood duck as the state waterfowl in 1974.

State fish: Largemouth, or black, bass Largemouth bass thrive in the warm waters of southern lakes and rivers. They may grow up to 22 pounds (10 kg). This bass is one of sportsmen's favorite game fish because of the fight it puts up when caught.

State insect: Honeybee Honeybees fly from flower to flower and help pollinate many fruits and vegetables. Without their help, some plants could not produce fruit and would eventually die out. Beekeepers in Mississippi keep hives of honeybees and sell the honey they produce. The honeybee was designated as the state insect in 1980.

State stone: Petrified wood
Mississippi's Petrified Forest in Madison County is the only forest of its kind east of the Rocky Mountains. Remnants of trees were apparently carried down a great prehistoric river 36 million years ago and buried in the sand and silt of Mississippi. In 1976, petrified wood was designated the state stone by a senate resolution.

State motto: *Virtute et armis* (By valor and arms)

State fossil: Prehistoric whale The prehistoric whale was designated the state fossil in 1981, after the fossilized bones of a zeuglodon, a whalelike animal, were unearthed in the state. ◼

Mississippi's State Song
"Go, Mississippi"

Words and music by Houston Davis

States may sing their songs of praise
With waving flags and hip-hoo-rays,
Let cymbals crash and let bells ring
'Cause here's one song I'm proud to sing.

(Choruses)
Go, Mississippi, keep rolling along,
Go, Mississippi, you cannot go wrong,
Go, Mississippi, we're singing your song,
M-I-S-S-I-S-S-I-P-P-I

Go, Mississippi, you're on the right track,
Go, Mississippi, and this is a fact,

Go, Mississippi, it's your state and mine,
M-I-S-S-I-S-S-I-P-P-I

Go, Mississippi, continue to roll,
Go, Mississippi, the top is the goal,
Go, Mississippi, you'll have and you'll hold,
M-I-S-S-I-S-S-I-P-P-I

Go, Mississippi, get up and go,
Go, Mississippi, let the world know,
That our Mississippi is leading the show,
M-I-S-S-I-S-S-I-P-P-I

CHAPTER EIGHT

Mississippi at Work

Farming, though still an important industry, is not as dominant as it once was in Mississippi.

C hange has come. Mississippi will never be last again!" announced Ray Mabus Jr. when elected governor of Mississippi in 1987. Mabus and his successor, Kirk Fordice, have worked to bring more industry to the state, improve education, and provide a more highly trained workforce. In the last decades of the twentieth century, Mississippi has overcome its past difficulties and is making strides toward a bright and prosperous future.

Employment

In the 1990s, unemployment declined in Mississippi as more than 140,000 new jobs were created. In 1997, the unemployment rate was just under 5 percent.

New businesses and industries have invested billions of dollars in the state. Service industries and manufacturing have become dominant. Farming and ranching, forestry, fishing, and mining—

Opposite: Unloading a fishing boat in Biloxi

once economic leaders in the state—provide the remainder of the state's income. In 1995, service industries provided more than 60 percent of the gross state product (GSP) of Mississippi. The GSP is the total of all goods and services produced in the state each year. Service industries employ nearly two-thirds of the state's labor force.

Mississippi boasts an ample labor force—more than 1.2 million workers. Average wages, however, are the lowest in the nation. Per capita income, a measure of the annual income earned by each person in the state, was $16,683 in 1995—well below the national figure of $23,208. In recent years, however, income has risen in Mississippi faster than the national average.

Service Industries

The service industries include wholesale and retail sales, government services, finance (banking and investment companies), insurance, real estate, health care, and public education. Mississippi's wholesale products include automobiles, farm and forest products, and petroleum. Retail trade, one of the state's leading employers, includes automobile dealerships, grocery stores, and restaurants.

Jackson is the center of Mississippi's financial operations. Most of the state's major insurance companies, real-estate firms, and banks are headquartered in the state's capital. Government agencies, primarily centered in Jackson, provide services throughout the state. These services include the operation of public schools, public hospitals, and military bases. Social-service agencies also provide assistance to many people.

Service industries operated by private citizens include law firms, repair shops, clinics, hotels, private hospitals, and doctors'

Service industries, such as real estate and insurance companies, have grown in importance.

offices. Transportation, communication, and utilities are also service industries, and Mississippi's location in the heart of the Southeast makes it an important center for these industries.

Transportation

There are about 73,000 miles (117,500 km) of highways in Mississippi. Several large cities have commercial airports with scheduled air service—Jackson International is the largest. Twenty railroads provide freight service, and passenger trains serve about fifteen cities.

Mississippi's numerous waterways carry much of the state's commercial transportation. The Gulf Coast's two major deepwater seaports, Gulfport and Pascagoula, handle millions of tons of cargo each year from U.S. and foreign ports. The Gulf Intercoastal Waterway protects coastal vessels from dangers of the open sea. Completed in 1949, this 1,065-mile (1,714-km) water route stretches along the Gulf Coast from Brownsville, Texas, to Carrabelle, Florida. It crosses Mississippi's coastline through the

Many barges filled with cargo travel along the Mississippi River.

Grand Gulf Nuclear Power Station

Mississippi Sound, the body of water between the state's mainland and its offshore islands.

The major inland commercial waterways are the Mississippi River and the Tennessee-Tombigbee Waterway, also known as the Tenn-Tom Waterway. The Mississippi River carries barges loaded with cargo to many inland states. Greenville, Natchez, Rosedale, and Vicksburg are the state's busiest river ports. The Tennessee-Tombigbee Waterway, on the east side of the state, is a man-made canal that connects the Tennessee and Tombigbee Rivers. The waterway provides cities in northeastern Mississippi and neighboring states to the north with direct access to the Gulf of Mexico.

Sources of Energy

Coal-burning power plants generate about 40 percent of Mississippi's electricity. A nuclear plant near Port Gibson provides an additional 40 percent. The Grand Gulf Nuclear Power Station began operation in 1985. It generates electricity from steam produced by the heat of nuclear fission.

Plants that burn natural gas also supply some of the state's electrical needs. In addition, Mississippi buys some of its electricity from the Tennessee Valley Authority (TVA), a federal corporation created in 1933 to develop the natural resources of the Tennessee Valley. Dams along the Tennessee River provide hydroelectric power to surrounding states.

Communications

Mississippi has 214 radio stations and twenty television stations. More than 150 newspapers are published in the state, including 28 daily papers and more than 100 weeklies. About thirty-five periodicals, mostly magazines, are published.

The oldest newspaper still published in Mississippi, the *Woodville Republican,* was founded in 1823. The dailies with the largest circulations include *The Sun Herald* of Biloxi and Gulfport, *The Clarion-Ledger* of Jackson, and the *Northeast Mississippi Daily Journal* of Tupelo.

Manufacturing

In the 1930s, Mississippi began its program to "balance agriculture with industry" (BAWI). As a result of this ongoing commitment, manufacturing continues to expand its share of the state's economic output. In 1991, the state only ranked twenty-third in the nation in the value of its manufactured goods, but manufacturing has become the foundation of its economic well-being.

In the 1950s, the apparel (clothing) industry replaced the lumber and wood-products industry as Mississippi's largest manufacturing employer. As a result of a boom in shipbuilding in the 1970s and an increase in auto-parts factories in the 1990s, the transportation-equipment industry is now the largest manufacturing

The Tenn-Tom Waterway

Vessels traveling south from Tennessee on the Tennessee River enter Pickwick Lake in far northeastern Mississippi. From there, commercial and pleasure craft can sail through a system of canals and locks extending 234 miles (377 km) to Columbus Lake, between Starkville and Columbus. From there, the Tombigbee River runs south to the Gulf.

The Tenn-Tom Waterway was completed in 1984 at a cost to the federal government of $2 billion. A total of 350 million cubic yards (268 million cu m) of earth had to be removed to build the waterway. That's nearly twice the amount of earth removed to build the Panama Canal, which makes Tenn-Tom the largest excavation project in history. ■

A shipbuilding company in Pascagoula

employer. The food and food-products industry, the electrical-equipment industry, and the furniture-making industry also employ a substantial share of Mississippi's workforce.

Cotton continues to be one of the state's most profitable crops.

Agriculture

The trends in Mississippi's agricultural industry usually follow the national trends. Employment declines as increased mechanization performs more and more of the farmworkers' tasks. Farm production increases, however, because of the increased efficiency of the machines.

Cotton and soybeans, Mississippi's most valuable crops, are grown mostly on the flat, fertile fields of the Delta. Farmers throughout the state grow hay, corn, and grain sorghum for livestock feed. Other crops are rice, wheat, and peanuts. In addition, Mississippi produces valuable amounts of cottonseed, pecans, and greenhouse and nursery products, such as flowers, houseplants, and seedling trees. The state's leading vegetables are sweet potatoes, cucumbers, and cowpeas. Mississippi's important fruits are peaches, watermelons, and muscadine grapes.

Poultry and Cattle

Poultry, especially broilers (chickens five to twelve weeks old), is important to Mississippi's agricultural economy. Poultry and eggs are the state's top agricultural commodity, earning $1.35 billion in 1996. Poultry farms and associated processing plants and distribution centers are located mainly in the south-central region of the state.

Beef cattle are raised in most areas of the state, except the Delta. Livestock raisers benefit from Mississippi's mild climate, which provides a long growing season for feed crops. Dairies are also scattered across the state. In 1995, dairy cattle produced 710 million pounds (320 million kg) of milk. Some livestock producers also raise pigs and sheep.

Forestry

Forests cover more than half the area of the state. Mississippi also has about 5,700 tree farms—more than any other state— and grows about 120 varieties of trees. The most important commercial varieties are the loblolly, longleaf, and slash pines of the Piney Woods area and the shortleaf pine of northern and central Mississippi. Other trees include ash, bald cypress, elm, hickory, pecan, sweet gum, cottonwood, and oak. Hardwoods, such as oak and hickory, supply material for the furniture-making industries. Pine softwoods are harvested as lumber and wood pulp for paper, fiberboard, and particleboard.

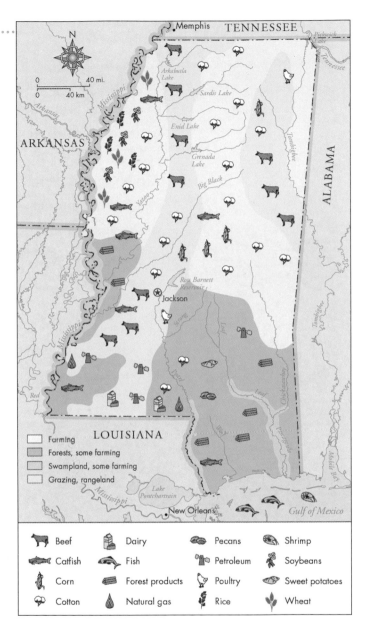

Mississippi's natural resources

Early in the twentieth century, Mississippi's forests were stripped by heavy harvesting. A reforestation program provided for new growth, however, and today, the "third forest" (third growth of trees) provides raw materials for several industries. Although employment in the forestry industry has been decreasing, lumber and wood products continue to be important to the state's economy.

Harvesting catfish

Catfish Farms and Fishing

Raising catfish in man-made ponds, which is called aquaculture, has become big business for farmers in the Delta. Mississippi is the nation's leading producer of farm-raised catfish. Sixty-five percent of the world's farm-raised catfish comes from Mississippi. The area around Belzoni is the center of this thriving industry. More than 100,000 surface acres (40,000 ha) of catfish ponds dot the landscape. As of 1997, slightly more than 1 billion catfish lived in Mississippi catfish ponds.

Mississippi has a thriving freshwater and saltwater fishing industry. The primary catch of the commercial marine (saltwater) fishery includes white trout, spotted sea trout, flounder, red drum, blue crab, red snapper, and mullet. Commercial vessels search for these species relatively close to land. In deeper waters farther offshore, the catch is mainly

Fried Catfish

Mississippi raises more catfish than any other state. This simple recipe makes the most of this southern specialty.

Ingredients:
  2 cups milk
  2 eggs, beaten
  1 teaspoon hot sauce
  1 cup cornmeal
  1/4 cup all-purpose flour
  2 tsp. salt
  4 catfish fillets
  vegetable oil

Directions:
Mix the milk, eggs, and hot sauce in a shallow bowl. Mix the cornmeal, flour, and salt in another shallow bowl. Dip the catfish fillets in the milk mixture, then in the cornmeal mixture. Evenly coat each fillet. Set the fillets aside on a plate.

Heat 2 inches of vegetable oil in a deep skillet until the oil starts to pop and sizzle. Ask an adult to fry the fillets. Cook one or two at a time, for two or three minutes on each side, until they are golden brown. Drain the fillets on paper towels, and they are ready to serve.

Serves four.

mackerel, lemonfish, bonito, marlin, bluefish, wahoo, sailfish, tuna, oysters, and shrimp.

The port at Pascagoula–Moss Point handles most of the commercial fishing trade. In 1991, it was the nation's fifth-largest commercial fishing port.

Tourism

Tourism, Mississippi's third-largest industry, produced $4.1 billion in 1995. Mississippi attracts hunters and fishers from around the world. In thirty-one state wildlife management areas and seven national wildlife refuges, there are more than 1 million acres (400,000 ha) of prime game land. Mississippi's six main reservoirs offer what may be the best fishing in the South. Several sports magazines rank Columbus Lake, along the Tennessee–Tombigbee Waterway, as "one of America's top twenty hot spots" for bass fishing.

The antebellum mansions and plantations, many in the Natchez and Vicksburg areas, are among the state's major attractions. Gulf Coast beaches lure visitors year-round due to the mild winter climate. Many tourists also visit the state fair, which is held in Jackson every year during the second week in October.

The Natchez Trace Parkway, Gulf Islands National Seashore, and Vicksburg National Military Park—three of the state's four national parks—attract the most visitors annually. For those eager to camp, there are six national forests, twenty-eight state parks, and numerous lakes.

Tourists come to see the state's historic homes and plantations.

Mining

Mining accounts for only 1 percent of the gross state product. Petroleum and natural gas make up about 90 percent of the value of the state's mined products. Petroleum production is heaviest in the southeastern and southwestern corners of the state. South-central Mississippi has many natural gas wells. Rankin County, just east of Jackson, produces one-fifth of the state's natural gas.

Ship Island National Seashore is an attraction for both tourists and natives.

What Mississippi Grows, Manufactures, and Mines

Agriculture	Manufacturing	Mining
Cotton	Food products	Petroleum
Broilers	Transportation equipment	Natural gas
Soybeans	Electrical equipment	
Beef cattle	Wood products	
Milk	Paper products	

A Success Story

Born in Canada in 1941, Bernard J. "Bernie" Ebbers came to Mississippi to play basketball for Mississippi College in Clinton. In 1983, he and a small group of Mississippi investors began to meet regularly in a Hattiesburg coffee shop to form a new long-distance company, LDDS (Long Distance Discount Service).

By 1985, Ebbers was the growing company's president. In 1995, LDDS changed its name to World-Com. That year, it appeared for the first time on *Fortune* magazine's list of the nation's largest companies. By the next year, the Jackson-based company had become the fourth-largest long-distance telecommunications company in the United States.

In 1997, WorldCom purchased MCI Communications, the second-largest long-distance carrier in the United States, for $37 billion—the biggest deal in U.S. corporate history. The combined company, MCI WorldCom, provides local, long-distance, and Internet services to 22 million customers throughout the world. ■

Mississippi's other mineral products include sand and gravel, clays, and crushed stone. The primary types of clay mined in the state are bentonite, used to lubricate oil well drills, and fuller's earth, used in refining oils and fats. Other clays include ball clay, kaolin, and common clays used to make bricks and tiles. Limestone quarries along the state's eastern border are the main source of crushed stone.

Fortune 500 Companies

Every year, *Fortune* magazine ranks the 500 most successful corporations in the United States. For a business, being included on the Fortune 500 list is as much of an honor as winning an Academy

Award is for an actor. More than 125 Fortune 500 industrial corporations have built factories, warehouses, or national headquarters in Mississippi. Huge companies like General Electric and Chevron are planning multimillion-dollar expansions to plants already in the state. Mazda North America selected Olive Branch in De Soto County as the site of a $20 million automotive-parts distribution center, the largest in the world.

Each day, the state welcomes more of these large companies. They are drawn to Mississippi because of its location, economic incentives, and ample workforce.

Whirlpool appliances and Peavey musical sound systems are among the many companies with headquarters in Mississippi.

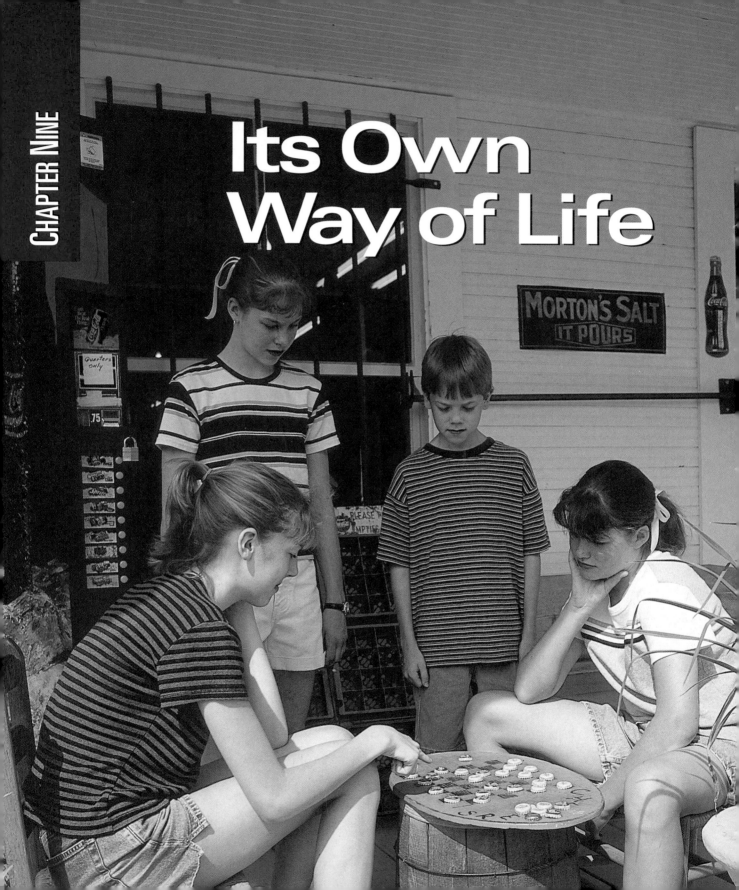

CHAPTER NINE

Its Own Way of Life

Traditionally, Mississippi's way of life has been rural and unhurried. Although the state continues to be more rural than urban, its lifestyle is no longer agrarian. Only 20 percent of rural dwellers actually live on farms. As large numbers of people have moved from farms to small towns and from small towns to cities, the way of life has begun to change.

Although Mississippi is still one of the most rural states in the United States, the urban population has increased dramatically. In 1920, only 13 percent of the state's residents lived in cities. In 1990, 47 percent of the population lived in urban areas, and 53 percent in rural areas.

In a 1990 census, Mississippi had a population of 2,586,443, ranking thirty-first among the fifty states. The metropolitan area of Jackson had a population of 395,000, ranking ninety-second in the nation. In 1996, the total population of Mississippi was estimated at 2,716,115—an increase of 6 percent since 1990.

Many Mississippians have moved from farms to small towns.

Opposite: Taking time to play checkers

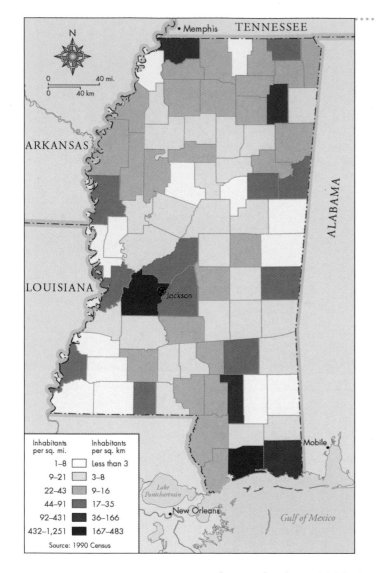

Mississippi's population density

Inhabitants per sq. mi. / Inhabitants per sq. km

1–8	Less than 3
9–21	3–8
22–43	9–16
44–91	17–35
92–431	36–166
432–1,251	167–483

Source: 1990 Census

A Mix of Peoples

According to the 1990 census, more than 99 percent of Mississippi's inhabitants were native-born U.S. citizens. Almost four-fifths were born within the state. Many white Mississippians are descendants of settlers from states along the Atlantic Seaboard and the Northeast and are primarily of Irish, Scots-Irish, English, German, French, and northern European ancestry. The state's black residents are, for the most part, descendants of slaves who were brought to Mississippi from West Africa in the eighteenth and nineteenth centuries.

From 1840 to 1940, the black citizens of Mississippi outnumbered the white. Although the 1980 census showed twenty-two counties in which there were more black inhabitants than white, the ratio of blacks to whites has declined continuously since 1900. In 1990, whites represented 64 percent of the population; blacks 35 percent; and other races, 1 percent. Even so, Mississippi has a higher percentage of African-American residents than any other state. Only the District of Columbia (Washington, D.C.) has a higher percentage.

Other groups in the state include Asian Americans, mostly of Chinese or Vietnamese origin; Pacific Islanders, mostly from the

Philippines; American Indians; and people of Hispanic descent. The small Chinese-American population (2,532 in 1990) in the Delta is made up of descendants of farm laborers brought to Mississippi from California in the 1870s. In 1990, there were 3,340 Vietnamese Americans and 2,120 Filipino Americans in Mississippi, drawn by the fishing industry and living almost entirely along the Gulf Coast.

About 9,000 Native Americans, mostly Choctaw, live in Mississippi. Most live on the Choctaw Reservation or in three surrounding east-central counties. People of Hispanic ancestry number about 16,000 and live throughout the state.

Choctaw Indians still live in Mississippi, mostly on their reservation.

Improving Education

For many years, Mississippi's public school system has ranked at the bottom of almost all measurable standards. Improvement of education has been a long-time goal in Mississippi, and there have been significant achievements in recent years.

Mississippi restructured its public education system after the state's historic Education Reform Act of 1982. The state had repealed the state's compulsory school-attendance law in 1956 to avoid complying with desegregation laws. After 1982, children between the ages of six and fourteen were again required to attend school. Statewide desegregation of schools did not begin until 1970. Today, all of the state's public school districts are integrated.

The state has also introduced competency testing of high school students, an appointed state school board, and an early childhood education program in attempts to improve the quality of education. According to the U.S. Department of Education, the public high

Population of Mississippi's Major Cities (1990)

Jackson	196,637
Biloxi	46,319
Greenville	45,226
Hattiesburg	41,882
Meridian	41,036
Gulfport	40,775

Oseola McCarty

Although she spent most of her life washing and ironing clothes for other people, in 1995, Oseola McCarty became a worldwide celebrity. She donated about 60 percent of her lifetime savings—$150,000—to the University of Southern Mississippi in Hattiesburg to establish a scholarship for African-American students. "I want to help somebody's child go to college . . . someone who will appreciate it and learn," she said.

Corporations and individuals have since contributed thousands of additional dollars to the fund. The first scholarship was awarded in August 1995, to Stephanie Bullock. In 1996, McCarty, who only completed the eighth grade, published *Oseola McCarty's Simple Wisdom for Rich Living,* a collection of her views about life. ▪

schools in Clinton and Tupelo have two of the best educational programs in the nation. Mississippi is also one of only five states to have a state-supported school devoted primarily to the study of mathematics and science on the secondary level. In "magnet" schools, students across the state have access to satellite-delivered instruction in foreign languages, mathematics, and science courses.

Jefferson College, founded in 1802, was one of the first public institutions of higher learning in the nation. In 1818, one of the nation's first women's colleges, Elizabeth Female Academy, was opened. The University of Mississippi, near Oxford, was chartered in 1844 and opened in 1848.

In addition to eight private and nine public colleges and universities, Mississippi has more than 100 vocational-tech-

The University of Mississippi near Oxford opened in 1848.

nical centers and 18 junior and community colleges. Other educational facilities include a medical center and the Gulf Coast Marine Research Laboratory.

Religion and Churches

There are more churches per capita in Mississippi than in any other state in the United States. More than 5,000 churches are found in the state. The majority of the churches are Protestant. Of the Protestant churches, Baptists and Methodists have the largest number of members. There are Jewish synagogues in the cities of Meridian, Greenville, Clarksdale, and Jackson.

During the state's tumultuous history, black congregations have relied on their churches as refuges from discrimination and racial hatred. The churches also provided a focus for families, bringing them closer in times of trouble. These churches, however, have also been easy targets for racist terrorism. Since the days of Reconstruction, arsonists—usually Ku Klux Klan members or members of other white supremacist groups—have bombed or burned hundreds of churches because they had black members. Throughout the 1990s, this violence

There are more than 5,000 churches in Mississippi.

Educational Firsts

There has been a long line of educational "firsts" in Mississippi. The Parent Teacher Association (PTA) was founded in the state in 1909. Mississippi was the first in the nation to have a system of junior colleges. The first land-grant college in the United States for African-Americans, Alcorn Agricultural and Mechanical College, now Alcorn State University, was established in Lorman in 1871. The first state-supported school for people with disabilities and the first coeducational college to grant degrees to women are both in Mississippi. ■

and destruction has continued in the churches of Mississippi and other parts of the South.

Mississippi Festivals

In Mississippi, the tradition of "getting together" is taken seriously. Family reunions, as well as annual events and festivals, provide many opportunities for spending leisure time with friends and family.

The Mule Festival is held in Jackson every spring, celebrating the animal's contribution to the state's settlement. Biloxi's Blessing of the Fleet, held every May for the past sixty years, is believed to ensure a bountiful shrimp harvest. The Mississippi Crossroads Blues Festival in Greenwood celebrates blues music and its importance to the state. Two Kudzu Festivals are held each year: one in Holly Springs in July and the other in Yazoo City in August.

Mississippi Sayings

In northern Mississippi, a creek is sometimes called a "burn," a burlap bag is called a "tow sack," and fireplace andirons are "dog irons." Cling peaches are "plum peaches," and dragonflies are called "snake doctors." People in southern Mississippi call a porch a "gallery," and they refer to dragonflies as "mosquito hawks."

"Fit to be tied" means "extremely upset." A person who wants to "get shed of" something wants to get rid of it. "To hanker" means "to want" something, but "to hunker" means "to stoop down." A "mess" of items and "a right smart" of them both refer to a large quantity. "Plumb" means "completely," and "old-timey" means "old-fashioned." If a person works hard for "a spell" (a while), he'll probably get "tuckered out" (tired). He might even get "stove up" (stiff and sore). ■

The International Balloon Classic in Greenwood in mid-summer and Natchez's Great Mississippi River Balloon Race in mid-October offer spectacular hot-air-balloon demonstrations and races. Christmas is heralded by Jackson's huge Mistletoe Marketplace during the first weekend in November. Mardi Gras on the Gulf Coast begins as early as January and continues until the day before Ash Wednesday. Many other fairs, shows, trade days, flea markets, and festivals give Mississippians the chance to celebrate every month of the year.

The Gulf Coast's Mardi Gras celebration is one of many festivals held in the state each year.

Chapter Ten

Artists and Athletes

William Faulkner in Oxford

From the blues to ballet, fishing to football, Mississippi has contributed to the culture, arts, and athletic scenes of the country and the world. The state has been the birthplace and hometown to many individuals with exceptional creative talent and physical skills. In addition, Mississippi's many centers for entertainment and varied pastimes provide enjoyment and enrichment to visitors and residents alike.

Novelists, Poets, and Playwrights

Mississippi has been home to hundreds of novelists, poets, and playwrights. Many have gained international fame while establishing a respected, regional literary form known as southern literature.

William Faulkner (1897–1962) was born in New Albany. His most famous works include *The Sound and the Fury* (1929) and *Absalom, Absalom!* (1936). The novelist wrote several of his works in the two-story house that is today a museum in Oxford. Faulkner received the Nobel Prize for Literature in 1949, the Pulitzer Prize for Fiction in 1955, and another Pulitzer in 1963. He is considered by many to be one of the finest writers in the English language.

Born in Jackson on April 13, 1909, Eudora Alice Welty was the second Mississippi author to receive the Pulitzer Prize for Fiction,

Opposite: Golf is just one of the leisure sports Mississippi has to offer.

Mississippi's Bestsellers

Many of today's bestsellers are written by authors from Mississippi. John Grisham (left), who grew up in Southaven, is the author of a string of popular novels, many of which have also become successful movies—such as *The Firm, The Pelican Brief,* and *The Client.*

Thomas Harris grew up in Rich, Mississippi, and attended Clarksdale High School. He is best known for the book *The Silence of the Lambs,* which was made into a film in 1991 and received five Academy Awards.

Greg Iles grew up in Natchez and majored in English at the University of Mississippi. His first two novels, *Spandau Phoenix* and *Black Cross,* were instant bestsellers. Other award-winning Mississippi authors include Elizabeth Spencer, Walker Percy, Willie Morris, and Pulitzer Prize-winners Richard Ford and Beth Henley. ■

Eudora Welty won the Pulitzer Prize for Fiction for *The Optimist's Daughter.*

which she won for *The Optimist's Daughter* (1969). Welty received the Presidential Medal of Freedom in 1980 and the National Book Foundation's Medal for Distinguished Contribution to American Letters in 1992. She was knighted by the French government in 1987 and awarded France's highest civilian award, the Legion of Honor, in 1996. She also received Mississippi's Lifetime Achievement Award for her more than fourteen books, sixty-nine book reviews, and numerous short stories. The state's largest public library is named for her.

Richard Nathaniel Wright (1908-1960) was born near Natchez. He was the first black novelist to achieve fame and fortune in the United States. Most of his thirteen novels are autobiographical and portray the hardships faced by young blacks in the United States. His most famous works are *Native Son,* published in 1940, and *Black Boy,* published in 1945.

Thomas Lanier Williams III (1911–1983) was born in Columbus, Mississippi. He later changed his name to Tennessee Williams.

Many of his plays, and the movies made from them, have won numerous awards. *Cat on a Hot Tin Roof* won the 1955 Pulitzer Prize for Drama and an Academy Award for Best Picture of 1958. Williams wrote sixty-five plays, two novels, sixty short stories, two books of poetry, an autobiography, and dozens of essays. He received the Kennedy Center Honors Award in 1979 and the Presidential Medal of Freedom in 1980.

Blues Artists

In the Mississippi Delta, a style of music now known as the blues was born on the plantation cotton fields in the antebellum South. Since the early twentieth century, people have come to Clarksdale and other Delta towns on Saturday night to listen to local musicians "sing the blues"—including such popular tunes as "Sometimes I Feel Like a Motherless Child" or "Hell Hound on my Trail." Some of the best-known Mississippi blues artists of past and present include Muddy Waters, W. C. Handy, Robert Johnson, and B. B. King.

Country Music Superstars

Country music, the traditional music of rural southern whites, has its roots among the pioneer settlers of the region. Many of them brought traditional songs and folk dances from England, Ireland, and Scotland. The sacred themes of religious music also had a great impact on the development of country music, as did the work songs and chants of railroad and steamboat workers.

Tammy Wynette (1942–1998), born in Tremont as Virginia Wynette Pugh, had more than thirty-five number-one hit songs and eleven number-one albums. Known as the First Lady of Country

Richard Wright was born near Natchez.

Country star Tammy Wynette

Music, Wynette earned numerous awards, including a Grammy in 1969 for her album *Stand by Your Man*.

Charles Frank "Charley" Pride was born in the town of Sledge in 1938. His first hit record, "The Snakes Crawl at Night," was released in 1964. Thirty-five number-one songs have followed, along with thirty-one gold singles, four platinum singles, and twelve gold albums. His awards include Country Music Association Male Vocalist of the Year, which he won in 1971 and 1972, and three Grammy Awards, which he won in 1971.

LeAnne Rimes is country music's newest sweetheart. Born in the town of Pearl on August 28, 1982, Rimes started her career by winning the television talent contest "Star Search." She is the youngest person ever nominated for a Country Music Association award. She received two Grammy Awards in 1997 for her album *Blue*: Best New Artist and Best Female Country Vocal Performance.

Elvis Presley was born in Tupelo and always remembered his Mississippi roots.

Rock and Rollers

Born in Tupelo on January 8, 1935, Elvis Aaron Presley was one of the most beloved performers of all time. In 1948, after two recordings—"That's All Right, Mama" and "Blue Moon of Kentucky"— his popularity skyrocketed. During his career, Presley made dozens of movies and sold millions of records. Elvis, who died on August 16, 1977 at his Graceland mansion in Memphis, is known as the King of Rock and Roll.

Three of the members of the short-lived hard-rock group Blind Melon, are from Mississippi. Drummer Glen Graham and bass guitarist Brad Smith are from Columbus. Guitarist Thomas Roger Stevens was born in West Point.

Musical Mississippians

Music Television Video (MTV) was the brainchild of Mississippian Bob Pittman. His 24-hour music-video channel first aired on August 1, 1981.

After graduating from Mississippi State University in 1965, Hartley Peavey of Meridian set out to manufacture electric guitar amplifiers. Today, Peavey Electronics Corporation produces amps, sound systems, and recording-studio equipment used by rock and roll, country, and blues bands throughout the world. ■

Opera

Jackson has two opera companies. The Mississippi Opera Association also brings opera to local universities and offers workshops and full-scale productions by local groups. Opera South, an integrated but predominantly black company, presents free operas during its summer tours and stages two major productions every year.

Leontyne Price, one of America's most beloved operatic sopranos, was born in Laurel on February 10, 1927. She attended the Juilliard School of Music in New York City, and her brilliant voice earned her international fame. In 1961, she appeared in Giuseppe Verdi's opera *Il Trovatore* in her Metropolitan Opera debut in New York City. In 1964, she was the first Mississippian to be awarded the Presidential Medal of Freedom, the nation's highest civilian award. She also received Mississippi's Lifetime Achievement Award, the highest honor of the Governor's Awards for Excellence in the Arts.

Eleni Matos, another opera star from Mississippi, was born in Jackson in 1966. She has won several competitions, including the Maria Callas International Opera Competition in Athens, Greece, and the International Luciano Pavarotti Competition. Matos is considered one of the world's rising opera stars.

Opera soprano Leontyne Price was born in Laurel.

William Grant Still

William Grant Still (1895–1978) was born in Woodville, Mississippi. Known as the dean of African-American composers, Still composed symphonies and shorter works that incorporate black and European musical styles. He was the first African-American composer to have a symphony performed by an American orchestra. He was also the first African-American to conduct a major symphony orchestra.

In 1949, Still became the first African-American to have an opera, *Troubled Island,* performed by a major opera company. In 1981, he was the first African-American to have an opera, *A Bayou Legend,* performed on national television. ■

Ballet and Theater

Jackson has two ballet companies and it is one of only four cities in the world to host the prestigious International Ballet Competition (IBC). IBC, founded in 1964, has been called the Olympics of Dance. Thalia Mara, a professional dancer and founder of the Jackson Ballet troupe, later called Ballet Mississippi, serves as the artistic director of the USA IBC. She brought the ballet competition to Jackson for the first time in 1979. In 1994, Jackson's Municipal Auditorium was officially renamed Thalia Mara Hall.

More than twenty community theaters are scattered throughout Mississippi. Established professional theater companies perform in Biloxi and Jackson. The New Stage, formerly called Jackson Little Theater and founded in 1925, is one of the oldest theater groups in the United States.

Sports Scene

The games of football, basketball, and baseball dominate Mississippi's sports scene, featuring college and university teams throughout the state. The biggest sports event of the year is the annual

On Stage, Film, and TV

Morgan Freeman, born in Memphis, has been nominated for three Academy Awards for his work in *Street Smart, Driving Miss Daisy,* and *The Shawshank Redemption.* He lives part-time on his ranch in Charleston, Mississippi.

James Earl Jones, born in Arkabutla, has starred in movies and Broadway plays. His distinctive voice is the voice of Darth Vader in the *Star Wars* movies and of Mufasa in Disney's *The Lion King.*

Ray Walston, born in Laurel, won the 1956 Tony Award for his role in the musical *Damn Yankees.* He has also appeared in many motion pictures and costarred in the 1960s TV series *My Favorite Martian.*

Oprah Winfrey (right) was born in Kosciusko. Her national television talk show, which has won thirty-two Emmy Awards, has made her name a household word, but she is also an accomplished actress. Winfrey received an Oscar nomination and a Golden Globe nomination for her role in *The Color Purple.* She also produced and starred in the 1998 film *Beloved,* based on the novel by Toni Morrison. ■

football showdown between the University of Mississippi Rebels and the Mississippi State Bulldogs. Mississippians have also won national college championships in tennis, men's and women's basketball, football, and men's soccer.

The Mississippi Sports Hall of Fame and Museum in Jackson is devoted to the sports celebrities of Mississippi. The museum offers a multi-screen video presentation, displays on the history of sports in the state, *Sports Illustrated* covers featuring Mississippians, and plaques for Hall of Famers, with biographical information on each person, along with artifacts and photographs.

Football Pros

Jerry Rice, whose hometown is Crawford, is considered to be the greatest wide receiver ever to play in the National Football League

NFL wide receiver
Jerry Rice is from
Crawford, Mississippi.

(NFL). Since 1985, he has played for the San Francisco 49ers, setting numerous NFL rushing and scoring records. He earned Most Valuable Player (MVP) awards for the 1989 Super Bowl game and the 1995 Pro Bowl game.

Walter Payton, a native of Columbia, played for the Chicago Bears from 1975 to 1987. The NFL's all-time leading rusher, with 16,726 yards (15,294 m), was inducted into the Pro Football Hall of Fame in 1993.

Archie Manning grew up in Drew and played college football for Ole Miss. He enjoyed an eleven-year career as a quarterback with the New Orleans Saints (1971–1982) before being traded to the Houston Oilers (1982–1983) and later to the Minnesota Vikings (1984). He was named National Football Conference (NFC) Player of the Year in 1978.

Other Mississippians who have played professional football include Brett Favre, quarterback of the Green Bay Packers, and L. C. Greenwood, a Canton native and two-time All-Pro for the Pittsburgh Steelers. Willie Brown, a Hall-of-Famer from Yazoo City, earned seven All-Pro titles during his sixteen-year career with the Denver Broncos (1963–1966) and the Oakland Raiders (1967–1978).

Baseball Greats

Several baseball legends began their careers in Mississippi. James Thomas "Cool Papa" Bell was probably the fastest runner ever to play baseball, circling the bases in twelve seconds or less. Born in Starkville on May 17, 1903, Bell played for various teams in the Negro League from 1922 until 1950. In 1974, he became the first native Mississippian inducted into the National Baseball Hall of Fame.

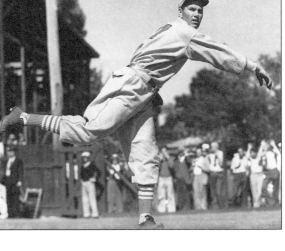

"Dizzy" Dean was raised in Bond and became famous as a pitcher.

Benoit's Archie Moore was a world-renowned boxer.

Jay Hanna "Dizzy" Dean was born in Arkansas on January 16, 1910. He grew up in Bond, Mississippi, and was baseball's most memorable pitcher during the Great Depression (1929–1940). Dean pitched for the St. Louis Cardinals in the 1930s, leading them to the World Series championship in 1934. He was traded to the Chicago Cubs in 1938 and retired from baseball in 1941. After his retirement, Dean became a popular TV sports commentator, broadcasting until his death in 1974. Dizzy Dean was inducted into the Baseball Hall of Fame in 1953.

Boxing Legends

Mississippi was the site of a significant event in the history of professional boxing. The last sanctioned bare-knuckles fistfight in the United States was fought at Richburg on July

8, 1889. John L. Sullivan defeated Jake Kilrain after seventy-five rounds.

In 1952, Archie Moore, born in Benoit, won the World Light-Heavyweight Championship. He defended his title eight times over the next ten years, winning a record number of bouts by knockouts. In 1990, Moore was inducted into the International Boxing Hall of Fame.

Columbus native Henry Armstrong is the only boxer to hold three world titles simultaneously: Featherweight (1937–1938), Lightweight (1938), and Welterweight (1938–1940). Armstrong was inducted into the International Boxing Hall of Fame in 1990.

Olympic Athletes

Mississippi's first Olympian was Donald M. Scott of Woodville. He competed in 1916, 1920, and 1924—the year he won the gold medal for the modern pentathlon. Mississippi State University's Scott Field is named after him.

Commodore and Roy Cochran, born in Richton, were the first brothers to win Olympic gold medals. Commodore (1902–1969) won in 1924 as part of the 1,600-meter relay team. Roy (1919–1981) won two gold medals in 1948: one in the 400-meter hurdles and one as a member of the 1,600-meter relay team.

Glen F. "Slats" Hardin, a native of Calhoun County, won the silver medal at the 1932 games and the gold medal in 1936, both for the 400-meter hurdles. Hayes Jones, a native of Starkville, won a gold medal in the 110-meter hurdles in the 1964 Summer Games. Swimmer Rowdy Gaines of Columbus won gold for the 100-meter freestyle event in the 1984 Olympics.

Ralph Boston, Mississippi's most decorated track athlete, was born in Laurel.

Superstar Willye B. White of Money, Mississippi, is the only female athlete to compete in five consecutive Olympic Summer Games, from 1956 to 1972. She won a silver medal for the long jump in 1956. She ran on the silver medal-winning USA team in the 4x100-meter relay in 1964.

Ralph Boston, a Laurel native, is Mississippi's most decorated track athlete. After winning the gold medal in the 1960 Olympics in Rome, he set world records in the long jump five times in the next five years. Boston won the Olympic silver medal in 1964 and the bronze in 1968.

Timeline

United States History

The first permanent British settlement is established in North America at Jamestown. **1607**

Pilgrims found Plymouth Colony, the second permanent British settlement. **1620**

America declares its independence from England. **1776**

The Treaty of Paris officially ends the Revolutionary War in America. **1783**

The U.S. Constitution is written. **1787**

Louisiana Purchase almost doubles the size of the United States. **1803**

United States and Britain **1812–15** fight the War of 1812.

The North and South fight **1861–65** each other in the American Civil War.

Mississippi State History

1540 Spanish explorer Hernando de Soto travels through the lands that are now Mississippi in search of gold.

1699 Pierre Le Moyne, Sieur d'Iberville, founds Old Biloxi, now Ocean Springs the first permanent white settlement in Mississippi.

1716 Jean Baptiste Le Moyne, Sieur de Bienville, establishes a second French settlement at Fort Rosalie, the site of modern Natchez.

1763 Great Britain wins the Mississippi region from France with its victory in the French and Indian War.

1781 Spain occupies the Gulf Coast.

1798 The Mississippi Territory is organized.

1817 On December 10, Mississippi becomes the twentieth state.

1822 Jackson becomes Mississippi's permanent state capital.

1861 Mississippi secedes from the Union.

United States History

The United States is **1917–18** involved in World War I.

The Stock market crashes, **1929** plunging the United States into the Great Depression.

The United States **1941–45** fights in World War II.

The United States becomes a **1945** charter member of the U.N.

The United States **1951–53** fights in the Korean War.

The U.S. Congress enacts a series of **1964** groundbreaking civil rights laws.

The United States **1964–73** engages in the Vietnam War.

The United States and other **1991** nations fight the brief Persian Gulf War against Iraq.

Mississippi State History

1863 Union forces capture Vicksburg after a forty-seven-day siege.

1877 Democrats gain control of the state legislature, and the Reconstruction era ends in Mississippi.

1927 Floodwaters from the Mississippi River kill hundreds of people and cause extensive property damage, causing the federal government to reroute the river.

1936 The Balance Agriculture with Industry (BAWI) program is initiated.

1962 James Meredith enrolls as the first black student at the University of Mississippi.

1963 Civil rights leader Medgar Evers is murdered.

1964 During Freedom Summer, volunteers throughout the country come to Mississippi to encourage African-American citizens to register to vote.

1969 A federal court orders the desegregation of Mississippi's public schools.

1989 Charles Evers, the brother of slain civil rights leader Medgar Evers, is elected mayor of Fayette, Mississippi. He is the first black mayor in the state since Reconstruction.

1991 Kirk Fordice becomes the first Republican to be elected governor since 1874.

Fast Facts

The capitol in Jackson

Statehood date	December 10, 1817, the 20th state
Origin of state name	Probably from the Ojibwa words *mici zibi,* which mean "great river" or "gathering of all the waters"
State capital	Jackson
State nickname	Magnolia State
State motto	*Virtute et armis* (By valor and arms)
State bird	Mockingbird
State flower	Magnolia
State fish	Largemouth bass
State shell	Oyster shell
State insect	Honeybee
State song	"Go, Mississippi"
State tree	Magnolia
State waterfowl	Wood duck
State land mammal	White-tailed deer
State water mammal	Bottlenosed dolphin
State fossil	Prehistoric whale

A magnolia blossom

Petrified wood

State stone	Petrified wood
State fair	Jackson (early October)
Total area; rank	48,286 square miles (125,061 sq km); 32nd
Land; rank	46,914 sq. mi. (121,507 sq km); 31st
Water; rank	1,372 sq. mi. (3,553 sq km); 22nd
Inland water; rank	781 sq. mi. (2,023 sq km); 27th
Coastal water; rank	591 sq. mi. (1,531 sq km); 10th
Geographic center	Leake, 9 miles (15 km) northwest of Carthage
Latitude and longitude	Mississippi is located approximately between 30° 13′ and 35° 00′ N and 88° 07′ and 91° 41′ W
Highest point	Woodall Mountain, 806 feet (246 m)
Lowest point	Sea level at the Gulf Coast
Largest city	Jackson
Number of counties	82
Longest river	Mississippi River
Population; rank	2,586,443 (1990 census); 31st
Density	54 persons per sq. mi. (21 per sq. km)
Population distribution	53% urban; 47% rural

**Ethnic distribution
(does not equal 100%)**

White	63.48%
African-American	35.56%
Hispanic	0.62%
Asian and Pacific Islanders	0.51%
Other	0.12%
Native American	0.33%

Mississippi River

Record high temperature	115°F (46°C) at Holly Springs on July 29, 1930
Record low temperature	–19°F (–28°C) at Corinth on January 30, 1966
Average July temperature	81°F (27°C)
Average January temperature	46°F (8°C)
Average annual precipitation	56 inches (142 cm)

Natural Areas and Historic Sites

National Battlefield Sites and Military Parks

Brices Cross Roads National Battlefield Site preserves the site of a Civil War battle.

Tupeolo National Battlefield is the site of a Civil War engagement in 1864.

Vicksburg National Military Park is the site of a forty-seven-day siege that ended in the surrender of the city to Union forces.

National Historical Parks

Natchez National Historical Park contains preserved antebellum architecture.

National Seashore

Gulf Islands National Seashore covers 135,625 acres (54,926 ha) along the Gulf Coast.

National Scenic Trail

Natchez Trace National Scenic Trail covers segments of the 694-mile (1,117-km) long trail that follows the Natchez Trace Parkway.

Natchez Trace
Parkway

Mississippi Gulf Coast

National Parkway

Natchez Trace National Parkway follows the historic route of Native Americans and early settlers from Mississippi to Tennessee.

State Parks

Mississippi had twenty-eight state park units in the late-1990s.

Sports Teams

NCAA Teams (Division I)

Alcorn State University Braves

Jackson State University Tigers

Mississippi State University Bulldogs

Mississippi Valley State University Delta Devils

University of Mississippi Rebels

University of Southern Mississippi Golden Eagles

Cultural Institutions

Jerry Rice

Libraries

Mississippi State Library (Jackson) is the oldest library in the state.

The University of Mississippi, Mississippi State University, and the *University of Southern Mississippi* all have academic libraries.

Museums

Lauren Rogers Library and Museum of Art (Laurel)

Mississippi Museum of Art (Jackson)

Meridian Museum of Art (Meridian)

Performing Arts

Mississippi has one major symphony orchestra, two ballet companies, and two opera companies.

University of
Mississippi

Universities and Colleges

In the mid-1990s, Mississippi had thirty-one public and sixteen private institutions of higher learning.

Annual Events

January–March

Dixie National Livestock Show and Rodeo in Jackson (February)

Mardi Gras festivities in various cities on the Mississippi Gulf Coast and in Natchez (February)

Garden Club Pilgrimages of Antebellum Homes in Aberdeen, Columbus, Holly Springs, Natchez, Port Gibson, Vicksburg, and other communities (March–April)

April–June

D'Iberville Landing and Historical Ball in Ocean Springs (April)

Natchez Trace Festival in Kosciusko (April)

Railroad Festival in Amory (April)

World Catfish Festival in Belzoni (April)

Atwood Bluegrass Festival in Monticello (May)

Jubilee Jam Art and Music Festival in Jackson (May)

Flea Market in Canton (May)

Jimmie Rodgers Memorial Festival in Meridian (May)

Civil War Reenactment in Vicksburg (May)

Blessing of the Fleet and Shrimp Festival in Biloxi (May)

Mississippi International Balloon Classic in Greenwood (June)

July–September

Choctaw Indian Fair in Philadelphia (July)

Mississippi Deep Sea Fishing Rodeo in Gulfport (July)

Watermelon Festival in Mize (July)

Crop Day in Greenwood (August)

Mardi Gras celebration

Choctaw Indian Fair

Neshoba County Fair in Philadelphia (August)

Delta Blues Festival in Greenville (September)

Seafood Festival in Biloxi (September)

October–December

Mississippi State Fair in Jackson (second week of October)

Natchez Fall Pilgrimage in Natchez (October)

Scottish Highland Games in Biloxi (November)

Christmas in Natchez (December)

Trees of Christmas Festival in Meridian (December)

Famous People

Jay Hanna "Dizzy" Dean (1910–1974)	Baseball player
Medgar Wiley Evers (1925–1963)	Civil rights leader
William Cuthbert Faulkner (1897–1962)	Author
Shelby Foote (1916–)	Novelist and historian
Jim Henson (1936–1990)	Puppeteer
Robert Johnson (1911–1938)	Musician
James Earl Jones (1931–)	Actor
Trent Lott (1941–)	U.S. senator
Walker Percy (1916–1990)	Novelist
Elvis Aaron Presley (1935–1977)	Singer
John C. Stennis (1901–1988)	U.S. senator
Muddy Waters (1915–1983)	Musician
Ida B. Wells (1862–1931)	Civil rights leader
Eudora Welty (1909–)	Author
Tennessee Williams (1911–1983)	Playwright
Oprah Winfrey (1954–)	Actress
Richard Wright (1908–1960)	Novelist
Tammy Wynette (1942–1998)	Country singer

Jim Henson

To Find Out More

History

- Coulter, Tony, et al. *La Salle and the Explorers of the Mississippi.* Broomall, Penn.: Chelsea House, 1981.

- Fradin, Dennis Brindell. *Mississippi.* Chicago: Childrens Press, 1995.

- Ready, Anna. *Mississippi.* Minneapolis: Lerner, 1993.

- Thompson, Kathleen. *Mississippi.* Austin, Tex.: Raintree/Steck Vaughn, 1996.

Fiction

- Fichter, George S., and Joe Boddy (illustrator). *First Steamboat Down the Mississippi.* Gretna, La.: Pelican Publishing, 1989.

- Holling, Holling C. *Minn of the Mississippi.* New York: Houghton Mifflin, 1992.

Biographies

- Coleman, Evelyn, Evelyn Daniel Minter, and Fred Willingham (illustrator). *The Riches of Oseola McCarty.* Morton Grove, Ill.: Albert Whitman, 1998.

- Medearis, Angela Shelf. *Princess of the Press: The Story of Ida B. Wells-Barnett.* New York: Lodestar, 1997.

- Miller, William, and Gregory Christie (illustrator). *Richard Wright and the Library Card.* New York: Lee and Low, 1997.

Websites

- **State of Mississippi Home Page**
  http://www.state.ms.us/
  Information on state government, travel, tourism, education, and much more

- **John C. Stennis Space Center**
  http://www.ssc.nasa.gov/
  Information on research and activities and events for visitors

- **Artcom Museum Tour: Mississippi**
  http://www.artcom.com/museums/ms.htm
  Links to the sites of major museums in Mississippi

Addresses

- **Mississippi Division of Tourism**
  P.O. Box 1705
  Ocean Springs, MS 39566
  For information on travel and tourism in Mississippi

- **New State Capitol Building**
  PO Box 1018
  Jackson, MS 39215-1018
  For information on Mississippi state government

Index

Page numbers in *italics* indicate illustrations.

Meet the Authors

Charles George earned his bachelor's degree in Spanish and History from Tarleton State University, Stephenville, Texas, in 1974. He taught Spanish and Advanced Social Studies for fifteen years on the high school level, then "retired" to write full time. He loves doing research.

Linda George earned her bachelor's degree in Elementary Education from the University of Texas at El Paso in 1971. She taught at the elementary school level for ten years. In 1979, she began her professional writing career.

"After gathering stacks of information on the state from dozens of books, magazines, and incredible Internet sites, we headed for Mississippi. For twelve days, we toured museums, antebellum homes, and historic sties, gathering bits of information we couldn't have found in reference materials. Everywhere we went,

Mississippians eagerly helped us locate the information we sought, and shared their feelings about the Magnolia state.

"At the Vicksburg National Military Park, we renewed our interest in the Civil War and dabbed at tears, reading verses of 'The Bivouac of the Dead,' by Theodore O'Hara, printed on markers throughout the cemetery.

"From Jackson to Natchez, we traveled the Natchez Trace and walked along sections of the original Trace, gaining insight to the

hardships suffered by thousands of people who literally carved the historic pathway from the land. Throughout the state, we were impressed with all the reminders of Mississippi's history."

Charles and Linda have authored more than two dozen nonfiction books for children and young adults. They live in Central Texas near the small town of Rising Star.

Photo Credits

Photographs ©:

81st Training Wing History Office: 45
AP/Wide World Photos: 124, 133 bottom (Rich Pedroncelli), 48 bottom, 49, 67, 70, 118 bottom, 123, 125 top, 127
Charles Sullivan: 43
Choctaw Tribal Archives: 76, 135 top
Corbis-Bettmann: 40, 44, 47, 48 top, 50, 71 top, 117, 118 top, 119 bottom, 121, 122, 125 bottom, 135 bottom (UPI), 28, 35, 37, 119 top
D. Donne Bryant Stock Photography: 7 top center, 46, 60, 78, 105, 112 bottom, 134 top
David J. Forbert: 6 bottom, 68, 77, 94, 107 bottom, 130 bottom, 92 top
David McEwen: 8, 61
David R. Frazier: 6 top left, 6 top center, 52, 53, 59, 62, 97, 108
Envision: 103 (Steven Needham)
Gamma-Liaison, Inc.: 120
Gene Ahrens: cover, 9, 104, 113
Hawkins Photography/Governor Kirk Fordice's Office: 85
James P. Rowan: 64
Mike Wann: 63, 79, 88, 109
Mississippi Department of Archives & History: 15, 19
Mississippi Gulf Coast Convention & Visitors Bureau: 116 (Ken Murphy), 82, 115, 133 top, 134 bottom

New England Stock Photo: 84, 130 top (J. Christopher), 98 (Jean Higgins), 7 top left, 24, 80 (Jim Schwabel), 99, 111 (Clyde H. Smith)
North Wind Picture Archives: 12, 16, 20 top, 22, 25, 31, 32, 34, 36
Schomburg Center for Research in Black Culture: 41
Stock Montage, Inc.: 18, 20 bottom, 27, 29, 30, 38
The Catfish Institute: 71 bottom (Lou Manna), 102 (Jon Simon)
Tom Till: back cover
Tony Stone Images: 2 (Michael Busselle), 89 (John Elk), 58, 131 bottom (Mark Green), 74 (Frederick Myers)
Travel Stock: 57, 73, 100 (Buddy Mays), 7 bottom, 92 bottom
Unicorn Stock Photos: 95 (Travis Evans), 13 (Jean Higgins), 83, 91 (Andre Jenny), 54, 132 (Ronald E. Partis)
University of Southern Mississippi: 112 top
Viesti Collection, Inc.: 6 top right, 55, 69, 96, 131 top (Joe Viesti)
Visuals Unlimited: 65 (Mark E. Gibson)
Whirlpool Corporation: 107 top
Maps by XNR Productions, Inc.